One Thing

Sam Storms

"The more I ponder the source and ground of all our lasting joy, the more convinced I become that Sam Storms is right. It's the Beauty of God. In all his gifts we are to see him. Especially in the gospel we are to see him. In all our seeing of the natural world we are to let our eyes run up the beam of beauty to the Original. Let Sam Storms guide you biblically and waken your heart to the Treasure of Christ who is the image of the Beauty of God."

John Piper
Pastor for Preaching and Vision,
Bethlehem Baptist Church

One Thing

Developing a Passion for the Beauty of God

Sam Storms

CHRISTIAN FOCUS

About the Author

Sam Storms, Ph.D., is president of Enjoying God Ministries, based in Kansas City, Missouri, where he devotes his time to writing, itinerant speaking, and providing resources for Christians through his Web site, www.EnjoyingGodMinistries.com. Before moving to Kansas City in the summer of 2004, Dr. Storms taught theology for four years at Wheaton College in Wheaton, Illinois. He has authored ten books and numerous articles for journals and Christian magazines. Sam and his wife Ann are the parents of two grown daughters and the grandparents of one grandson.

Scripture quotations are from *The Holy Bible, English Standard Version*, copyright © 2001 by Crossway Bibles, a division of Good News Publishers. Used by permission. All rights reserved.

© Enjoying God Ministries, 2004

ISBN 1-85792-952-7

Published in 2004,
Reprinted 2004
by
Christian Focus Publications Ltd
Geanies House, Fearn, Ross-shire,
IV20 ITW, Scotland, Great Britain.

www.christianfocus.com

Cover Design by Alister MacInnes
Printed and Bound by MacKays of Chatham

Contents

Affectionately dedicated to

MIKE BICKLE

A man of one thing, in whose life I've seen a relentless passion for God that has challenged and encouraged me more than any other.

Thanks, dear friend!

Psalm 27: 4

One thing have I asked of the LORD,
that will I seek after:
that I may dwell in the house of the LORD
all the days of my life,
to gaze upon the beauty of the LORD
and to inquire in his temple.

'Father in heaven! What is a man without Thee! What is all that he knows, vast accumulation though it be, but a chipped fragment if he does not know Thee! What is all his striving, could it even encompass a world, but a half-finished work if he does not know Thee: Thee the One, who art one thing and who art all! So may Thou give to the intellect, wisdom to comprehend that one thing; to the heart, sincerity to receive this understanding; to the will, purity that wills only one thing. In prosperity may Thou grant perseverance to will one thing; amid distractions, collectedness to will one thing; in suffering, patience to will one thing. Oh, Thou that giveth both the beginning and the completion, may Thou early, at the dawn of day, give to the young man the resolution to will one thing. As the day wanes, may Thou give to the old man a renewed remembrance of his first resolution, that the first may be like the last, the last like the first, in possession of a life that has willed only one thing' (Søren Kierkegaard).

Purity of Heart Is To Will One Thing, Søren Kierkegaard, translated from the Danish with an Introductory Essay by Douglas V. Steere (New York: Harper Torchbooks, 1956), p. 31.

Chapter One

A Christian 'Theory of Everything'

For from him and through him and to him are all things.
To him be glory forever. Amen.

Romans 11:36

He was shockingly thin, often wore a powdered wig, and is known to most people for his graphic portrayal of the horrors of hell. But in the summer of 1723, at only nineteen years of age, puritan pastor Jonathan Edwards uttered the words that forever changed my life.

In that short statement he proved yet again that concise, poignant assertions, not long speeches or complex dissertations, have a strange power over the human soul. They inspire acts of remarkable courage. They motivate otherwise selfish people to deeds of indescribable sacrifice. They can turn hate to love, yet tragically, love to hate, as well. Sometimes they even turn the course of history.

I still struggle for words to describe the pervasive impact of Edwards' words. Little, if anything, in my life was left untouched.

What I thought was pleasing to God and what he wanted of me was forever transformed. Reading the Bible suddenly became a heartwarming adventure rather than a tedious discipline. I had to discard a good bit of what I thought was Christianity and rebuild from the ground up. My value system got turned on its head. I scrapped not only *why* but *how* I used to worship, and started over. The way I view the world and people and life's ultimate purpose experienced a serious and significant overhaul.

It's not the sort of thing you'd read in *People* magazine or hear on an episode of *Seinfeld*. As best I can tell it isn't well known. I don't expect to find it inscribed on a monument or printed on a T-shirt. It's too long for a bumper sticker but too short for a speech. When you first read it you may wonder why I'm so passionate about its truth and its capacity to transform how you think and feel and live and worship and pray and relate with other people. You won't find it in the Bible, but it's thoroughly biblical. Here it is:

> *Now what is glorifying God, but a rejoicing at that glory he has displayed? An understanding of the perfections of God, merely, cannot be the end of the creation; for he had as good not understand it, as see it and not be at all moved with joy at the sight. Neither can the highest end of creation be the declaring God's glory to others; for the declaring God's glory is good for nothing otherwise than to raise joy in ourselves and others at what is declared.*[1]

The style's a bit bumpy at first, but go back and read it again. Don't let the puritan prose throw you. If you're still confused let me unravel it for you with my modern paraphrase:

> *God is the most God-centered being in the universe. He is consumed with love for himself and has infinite*

admiration for his own beauty. This passionate desire to be joyfully celebrated is the reason you and I exist. If all we do is think about God, even if our thoughts are accurate, we're better off not thinking at all. Telling others what we think isn't much better. The reason why we think about God and tell others what we've thought is so that all of us might relish the very idea of Him and rejoice that so great a God is actually ours.

Gladness in God's Glory

I doubt you'd be reading this book if it were not your aim in life to glorify God. We don't always say it in so many words but, if pressed to define the meaning of life or our reason for being, followers of Jesus end up with some version of God's glory as the ultimate explanation for what they do and why. I can't imagine a Christian giving a different answer. If asked for biblical support, we're usually pretty good at citing texts like these:

- So, whether you eat or drink, or whatever you do, do all to the glory of God (1 Cor. 10:31).
- . . . to him be glory in the church and in Christ Jesus throughout all generations, forever and ever. Amen (Eph. 3:21).
- To the King of ages, immortal, invisible, the only God, be honor and glory forever and ever. Amen (1 Tim. 1:17).

But for many of these same people, 'glorifying God' is an empty shell. Ask them to describe what it means and you're likely to get a blank and embarrassed stare. Ask them to explain how it's actually *done* and they'll suddenly remember they're late to pick up Johnny from soccer practice and make a hasty exit. Glorifying God has become something of a mantra in the evangelical world. If you can affirm it often enough and with apparent spiritual intensity it's supposed to make routine problems disappear.

I'm not saying these people are hypocrites, as if they profess to glorify God without the conscious intent to do so. A hypocrite wants to impress others with an external façade of religious piety that he knows is devoid of internal spiritual substance. However, in most cases, otherwise sincere Christians simply don't know because either they've never been taught or they're rarely challenged to think deeply on what a life that glorifies God is supposed to look like.

So we'll assume there is at least a verbal consensus among Christians that creation exists for God's glory. But that's only step one. We're now faced with an even more important question: *How is he most glorified in us? Where and in what way is God's glory most clearly revealed? Through what mechanism or means do we bring him the honor that we all agree he deserves?* I believe the consistent answer of Scripture is that God is most glorified in us when our knowledge and experience of him ignite a forest fire of joy that consumes all competing pleasures and he alone becomes the treasure that we prize. Here's how Edwards puts it:

> God is glorified not only by his glory's being seen, but by its being rejoiced in. When those that see it delight in it, God is more glorified than if they only see it. God made the world that he might communicate, and the creature receive, his glory . . . both [with] the mind and the heart. He that testifies his having an idea of God's glory [doesn't] glorify God so much as he that testifies also his approbation [i.e., his heartfelt commendation or praise] of it and his delight in it.[2]

I'm not suggesting that understanding the nature of God isn't essential. Of course it is! Theological ignorance won't take us very far, at least not in the right direction. Excitement uninformed by truth invariably leads either to idolatry or fanaticism. If we don't know the God we enjoy, we may end up enjoying the wrong god! But knowledge alone isn't enough. Declaring God's glory to others is also important but, again, there's something even more fundamental to our existence. For evangelicals who've been raised to believe that theological precision is an end in itself, this may be a hard pill to swallow. For others who've reduced Christianity to obedience, it may sound self-indulgent.

My point is simply that *passionate and joyful admiration of God, and not merely intellectual apprehension, is the aim of our existence.* If God is to be supremely glorified in us it's critically essential that we be supremely glad in him and in what he has done for us in Jesus. So, here's why you *are*: to *relish and rejoice in the revelation of divine beauty.*

Created for Happiness

Let me begin to unpack this by appealing once again to something Edwards said. In a sermon entitled 'Nothing upon Earth can Represent the Glories of Heaven,' he makes another breathtaking assertion. 'God,' said Edwards, 'created man for nothing else but happiness. He created him only that he might communicate happiness to him.'[3] This seems to run against the grain of everything we've been taught. How can God have created us for *our* happiness if he created us for *his* glory? The two ideas appear to conflict at every turn. Don't liberals affirm the former and fundamentalists the latter? But who in their right mind would dare affirm both?

In fact, these are not different aims or mutually exclusive assertions. God created us to glorify himself by enriching us with the joy that flows from a saving encounter with the splendor of his Son. So the goal of our creation was not simply that we might be happy, but happy in beholding God's own eternal excellencies. Not in beholding our own accomplishments. Not in the enjoyment of our own sensual appetites. Not in the development of a healthy self-esteem or in the acquisition of a four-bedroom home with a three-car garage. *God* is the fountain of all felicity'[4] and bids us come and drink!

Many Christians today are horribly out of touch with this truth. They aren't resistant to joy, but they're more than a little suspicious of it. The problem is that they are oblivious to the beauty of God. Worse than that, they're bored. God is real to them. They're not atheists. He just isn't relevant. Far less is he cause for celebration. That's why when life is hard and disillusionment sets in, God isn't the first thing to enter their minds (if they think of him at all). Many instinctively turn to whatever will anesthetize their pain or bring a spark to their souls.

The reason for this isn't hard to see. The human soul wasn't created for boredom. We were shaped by God for the excitement that the revelation of his glory induces. We were fashioned for the fascination that the display of his goodness evokes. We were made for the happiness that the sweetness of Christ's tender mercies alone can impart. That doesn't sound boring to me!

An Important Definition

Happiness is an explosive and dangerous word. If I don't define it carefully I risk losing a lot of my readers who will mistake this book for countless others on the market that exchange the offense of the cross for shallow self-fulfillment.

When I speak of human happiness I'm not talking about physical comfort or a six-figure salary or emotional stability or the absence of conflict or sexual gratification or any such earthly or temporal achievement. That's not to say such things are inherently wrong. In their proper place they may well be expressions of divine benevolence. But we greatly err if they become foundational to human happiness. We should be grateful for them, but happiness is still within our grasp despite their absence.

The happiness for which we are eternally destined is a state of soul in which we experience and express optimum ecstasy in God. Happiness is the whole soul resting in God and rejoicing that so beautiful and glorious a Being is ours. Happiness is the privilege of being enabled by God's grace to enjoy making much of him forever. I'm talking about the ineffable and unending pleasure of blissful union with and the joyful celebration of Father, Son, and Holy Spirit. This is a joy of such transcendent quality that no persecution or pain or deprivation can diminish, nor wealth or success or prosperity can enhance. It's what Paul had in mind in Philippians 4:11 when he spoke of a satisfaction in Christ that was beyond the reach of either adversity or abundance.

Happiness defined

Everyone pursues happiness. We're all committed to squeezing out of life maximum pleasure and a minimum of pain. For many, life is little more than a frantic effort to minimize discomfort while holding on to the slim hope that somewhere along the way a measure of joy might be found. The lie we must combat is that money and cocaine and chocolate and a fully equipped SUV can do what God can't. One goal in writing this book is to persuade you that it is eminently reasonable to seek your joy in Jesus, that nothing is more sensible or more conducive to your temporal and eternal welfare than the sweetness of relishing the Son of God above all worldly enticements.

You weren't created to be a lawyer or school teacher or factory worker or football player. That's what you *do* to *make* a living, but it's not the reason for *living*. You were made to re-joice at the display of God's glory in Jesus Christ. In the first formal sermon he ever preached, Edwards put it this way:

> *The pleasures of loving and obeying, loving and ador-ing, blessing and praising the Infinite Being, the Best of Beings, the Eternal Jehovah; the pleasures of trusting in Jesus Christ, in contemplating his beauties, excellencies, and glo-ries; in contemplating his love to mankind and to us, in contemplating his infinite goodness and astonishing loving-kindness; the pleasures of [the] communion of the Holy Ghost in conversing with God, the maker and governor of the world; the pleasure that results from the doing of our duty, in acting worthily and excellently; ... these are the pleasures that are worthy of so noble a creature as a man is.[5]*

This revolutionary concept of Christianity is not unique to Edwards or the Reformed tradition he represents. One other example will suffice to make the point. John Wesley, founder of Methodism and a theological Arminian, came to the same conclusion:

> *One design you are to pursue to the end of time—the enjoyment of God in time and in eternity. Desire other things so far as they tend to this: love the creature, as it leads to the Creator. But in every step you take, be this the glorious point that terminates your view. Let every affection, and thought, and word, and action, be subordinate to this. Whatever you desire or fear, whatever you seek or shun, whatever you think, speak, or do, be it in order to your happiness in God,—the sole end, as well as source, of your being.[6]*

Wesley's point is unmistakable. The purpose of existence is the pursuit of enjoyment . . . in God! Our desires, affections, pursuits, all that we say and do, all that we love or hate, are to be measured by this single criterion and subordinated to this one end: happiness in God.

Your choice isn't *whether* to passionately seek pleasure. Trust me, you do (as I hope to make clear in chapter two). Your only option is where you'll look or whom you'll love or whose offer of pleasure you'll accept. I hardly need remind you, or perhaps I do, that the world will do everything in its power and employ whatever means necessary and spare no expense to capture the allegiance of your heart. I saw a perfect illustration of this recently at a local theater.

I arrived about thirty minutes early to view the new film *Luther* (a fairly accurate portrayal of the sixteenth-century reformer, I might add). What flashed before my eyes on the screen was a testimony to the relentless assault launched every day on the souls of unsuspecting men and women. It reminded me that corporate America knows something about the human soul that the church has yet to fully grasp: people are desperate for something, anything, that will bring excitement and energy to their otherwise bored existence, and most of them are willing to pay whatever it takes, no matter how painful or pricey, to get it. Colorful ads, slick announcements, and a half-dozen previews of coming attractions, pummeled the audience with a dizzying array of solutions to their struggles or the promise of an experience certain to satisfy their soul: there were science fiction fantasies, military adventures, the intrigue of Nintendo, sex, horror, a new thrill ride at Disney, more sex, romantic adventures, comedies for both old and young, music videos bizarre beyond words, athletic challenges, sex again, and even the occasional web-site of a church insisting that 'God does it better'; if that weren't enough, it comes with coke and popcorn and the opportunity to buy on-line your ticket for the next installment.

It was a vivid microcosm of what has become a global conspiracy to seduce the human soul with cheap and empty pleasures.

You weren't created for boredom or burnout or bondage to sexual lust or greed or ambition but for the incomparable pleasure and matchless joy that knowing Jesus alone can bring. Only then, in him, will you encounter the life-changing, thirst-quenching, soul-satisfying delight that God, for his glory, created you to experience.

'Apatheism'

'"Apatheism"? You mean "atheism", don't you?' No, I mean apatheism. I'd never heard the word either, until a few months ago. But it's important because it expresses an approach to life that is the absolute antithesis of everything this book is about.

I was browsing through Borders' bookstore and picked up the May, 2003, issue of *Atlantic Monthly* magazine. On page 34, Jonathan Rauch, 'an unrepentantly atheistic Jewish homosexual' (that's how he describes himself), defines 'apatheism' as 'a disinclination to care all that much about one's own religion, and an even stronger disinclination to care about other people's.' An atheist, says Rauch, cares deeply about religion, but in the opposite direction from an evangelical Christian. An 'apatheist', on the other hand, quite simply couldn't care less about anyone's religion, least of all his own.

Rauch believes that apatheism is the answer to the sort of religious zeal that produced 9/11 as well as the religious passion that energized people's response to it. 'Apatheism' doesn't come easily, though. We're not talking about being religiously lazy. 'Apatheism' is the fruit of a disciplined and determined effort to master one's spiritual passions. 'Apatheists' can be atheists, agnostics, or even church-going theists. The important thing is that they 'are neither controlled by godly passions nor concerned about the (nonviolent, noncoercive) religious beliefs of others.' Rauch is ecstatic about what he sees as the growth of apatheism in American society.

What you will discover in this book is a concentrated attempt to destroy apatheism. I want to arouse spiritual passion. I aim to pour as much gasoline on whatever is left of the lingering spark in your soul as I possibly can. I hope to stoke the fires of concern and zeal and yearning that God first lit in you when he shaped you in his image. I want you to care deeply and doggedly about your religion and to be disturbed and broken-hearted when others thumb their collective noses at Jesus.

Apathy is impossible in the presence of the Son of God. Ineffable beauty compels a response: either passionate devotion or hatred. Middle-of-the-road, straddle-the-fence, you-do-your-thing-and-I'll-do-mine indifference dies when Jesus draws near. Love him or despise him, but abandon the myth that he can be tolerated. Sing for joy or spit in his face. Apathy simply isn't an option.

I do have to give Rauch credit for one thing. He's right when he says that 'even regular churchgoers can, and often do, rank quite high on the apatheism scale'. How true, yet how tragic! But God created you for something better, for the heart-pounding joy and mind-bending fascination and white-hot happiness that comes from relishing and rejoicing in the beauty of Jesus Christ.

A Christian 'Theory of Everything'

Physicists and cosmologists are ever in search of what they call 'a theory of everything', or a T.O.E., a hypothesis that is all-encompassing in its explanatory power, a theory that can account for both the sub-atomic world of particle physics and the galactic expanse of supernovae and black holes.

Brian Greene, professor of physics and mathematics at Columbia University, is the author of a fascinating book entitled, *The Elegant Universe*. Greene argues that 'for the first time in the history of physics we ... have a framework with the capacity to explain every fundamental feature upon which the universe is constructed.'[7] Scientists call it *string theory,* and I talk more about it in chapter six. The idea is that everything in the universe at its most microscopic level consists of combinations of vibrating strings. According to Greene, 'string theory provides a single explanatory framework capable of encompassing all forces and all matter.'[8]

The problem isn't that Greene and others have gone too far in making this claim. The problem is they haven't gone nearly far enough! Greene is clearly drawn to this theory because strings make sense of physical reality in all its manifold dimensions. But what makes sense of strings? Why do *they* exist? Scientists may well be correct about the capacity of strings 'to explain every fundamental feature upon which the universe is constructed'. But why strings? If they explain all forces and all matter, *what explains them*? What accounts for the shape they take and the functions they serve? God does!

This book is about a *Christian* T.O.E. My theory is that everything, what Greene refers to as 'all forces and all matter', exists for the glory of God or, to use words that I will later unpack, *the manifestation of divine beauty*. Let me emphasize the E. in T.O.E. and say again that *everything* from quarks to quasars, from butterflies to baseballs, were created and are sustained so that you and I might delight in the display of divine glory. Only humans are fashioned in the image of God.

We alone have been endowed with the capacity to glorify him by *rejoicing* in the beauty of his creative handiwork and *relishing* the splendor of his self-revelation in the person and redemptive work of his Son.

We're touching here on the most profound question anyone could ever ask: *Why is there something rather than nothing?* Why is there a 'me', a 'you', an 'us'? In an otherwise intriguing book, *A Short History of Nearly Everything*, Bill Bryson tries to answer that question without appealing to God or a grand purpose. There was a time, says Bryson, when 'there were no atoms and no universe for them to float about in. There was nothing—nothing at all anywhere.'[9] He admits that 'it seems impossible that you could get something from nothing, but the fact that once there was nothing and now there is a universe is evident proof that you can.'[10] For Bryson, it's more reasonable to assert the 'impossible' and logically absurd than to acknowledge the existence of an eternal Creator. Talk about a leap of faith!

And what about you and me? Why are we 'somethings'? I doubt you'll find Bryson's answer encouraging, but here it is: 'Even a long human life adds up to only about 650,000 hours. And when that modest milestone flashes past, or at some other point thereabouts, for reasons unknown your atoms will shut you down, silently disassemble, and go off to be other things. And that's it for you.'[11] The best you can hope for is the opportunity to enjoy the short ride of existence while it lasts. You came out of nothing and you are going into nothing. End of story.

Samuel Beckett took hold of this perspective and put it on stage in 1969. His thirty-five-second play, *Breath*, is one of the most pointed and undeniably bizarre attempts to express the meaninglessness of life that I know of. There are no human participants in this play. No heroes, no villains. No plot, no progression. The curtain is slowly raised, revealing a pile of garbage on the stage, offensive to both sight and smell. No words are spoken. There is only a dim light, accompanied by a baby's shrill cry of pain and an inhaled breath. The light increases somewhat and then recedes into darkness. The play ends as it began, with the loud cry of an aged man and his dying gasp. And the curtain falls. End of story.

Such is life and its 'purpose' (if the word is even appropriate). It emerges out of darkness, is birthed in anguish, lasts for but a breath, and consists of refuse. The end is as the beginning. A transient breath, more pain, and a return to darkness.

Christians have a different (and dare I say more reasonable, not to mention more pleasing) explanation for why there is something rather than nothing. God made us. But why did God choose to create? Certainly not from the anguish born of need, as if creation might supply God what he lacked. God didn't take inventory and suddenly realize there was a shortage that only you and I could fill up. So what prompted God to act?

I hope you like this as much as I do: The source of God's creative energy was the joy of infinite and eternal abundance! *God chose to create from the endless and self-replenishing overflow of delight in himself.* That needs to be said again. *God chose to create from the endless and self-replenishing overflow of delight in himself.*

We have to begin with the recognition that God delights infinitely in his own eternal beauty. When God the Father beholds himself in the Son he is immeasurably happy. He gazes at the Son and sees a perfect reflection of his own holiness. The Father rejoices in the beauty of the Son and Spirit, and the Son revels in the beauty of the Spirit and Father, and the Spirit delights in that of the Father and Son. God is his own fan club!

This benevolent fullness of divine delight overflows in creation so that we might joyfully share, to God's eternal glory, in God's admiration of himself.

God created us so that the joy he has in himself might be ours. God doesn't simply think about himself or talk to himself. He *enjoys* himself! He celebrates with infinite and eternal intensity the beauty of who he is as Father, Son, and Holy Spirit. And we've been created to join the party!

My principal aim in this book is to convince you that nothing is more important than understanding this truth. Not simply important for your intellectual development or to satisfy your theological curiosity or to overcome 'apatheism' in your soul, but crucial for the quality of your existence now and in the age to come. Bryson's right about one thing: human existence on this earth is terribly brief, a mere 650,000 hours (and somewhat less for a lot of people). But contrary to his prognosis, for 'reasons' made clear in Scripture our atoms, following death, will be supernaturally 'reassembled' as we are resurrected and glorified for an eternity of indescribable bliss! If this T.O.E. is true, we can hardly expect to experience the abundance of life of which Jesus spoke (John 10:10) and died to obtain and rose again to impart if we persist in ignorance of God's creative design and how it touches every fiber and fabric of our being.

To relish and rejoice in the beauty of God alone accounts for why we exist. It's also the solution to our struggle with sin. Enjoying God is the catalyst for substantive and lasting change. And enjoying God is the soul's sole satisfaction, with which no rival pleasure can hope to compete. Glorifying God by enjoying him forever. It's the Christian Theory of Everything.

A Preview

Let me provide a brief preview of where we're going. I can hardly expect you to embrace pleasure in God as a legitimate ambition, much less as a cogent T.O.E., if you are suspicious of pleasure itself. In chapter two I briefly articulate a philosophy of life known as Christian Hedonism in which not merely the *discovery* of God but *delight* in him is foundational to our very existence and thus crucial to all decision-making.

In chapters three through six my focus is God, not as you've come to expect him, but God in the manifold display of his ineffable beauty, both in creation and redemption. I then turn, in chapters seven and eight, to the practical payoff. These are the 'so what' chapters in which I explain the catalytic power of our encounter with divine beauty. I conclude in chapter nine with a description of the consummation of our gladness in God as it will unfold in ever-increasing intensity in heaven.

We live in a different world since 9/11. Patriotism energized us for a while. There was even a momentary increase in church attendance. But honest folk will admit that cynicism and fear now often dictate how they live, and they're terrified to think that it's not going to change anytime soon. Our only hope is to synchronize our souls to harmonize with God's ultimate creative design. To this end we must enjoy him. But to enjoy him we must know him. So let's begin.

---

[1] Jonathan Edwards, *The Miscellanies (Entry Nos. a-z, aa-zz, 1-500)*, The Works of Jonathan Edwards, Volume 13. Edited by Thomas A. Schafer (New Haven: Yale University Press, 1994), no. 3, p. 200.

[2] Ibid., no. 448, p. 495.

[3] Jonathan Edwards, *Sermons and Discourses 1723-1729,*

The Works of Jonathan Edwards, Volume 14. Edited by Kenneth P. Minkema (New Haven: Yale University Press, 1997), pp. 145-46.

[4] Ibid., p. 151.

[5] Jonathan Edwards, 'Christian Happiness' in *Sermons and Discourses 1720-1723*, The Works of Jonathan Edwards, Volume 10. Edited by Wilson H. Kimnach (New Haven: Yale University Press, 1992), pp. 305-06.

[6] John Wesley, *A Plain Account of Christian Perfection* (Peterborough, U.K.: Epworth Press, 1997), pp. 7-8.

[7] Brian Greene, *The Elegant Universe: Superstrings, Hidden Dimensions, and the Quest for the Ultimate Theory* (New York: W. W. Norton & Company, 1999) p. 16.

[8] Ibid., p. 15.

[9] Bryson, *A Short History of Nearly Everything* (New York: Broadway Books, 2003), p. 2.

[10] Ibid., p. 13.

[11] Ibid., p. 2.

Chapter Two
Confessions of a Christian Hedonist
Oh, taste and see that the Lord is good!

Psalm 34:8

I am a Christian hedonist. I think it's important you know this about me right from the start. Some will find it strange that I use such language while others may be offended. So let me explain. I'm a *hedonist* because I believe it is impossible to desire pleasure too much. But I'm a *Christian* hedonist because I believe the pleasure we cannot desire too much is pleasure in God and all that he is for us in Jesus.

Let me go even further and say that when it comes to satisfying our spiritual appetites, *there is no such thing as excess.* There are no restraints placed on us by God. There are no rules of temperance or laws requiring moderation or boundaries beyond which we cannot go in seeking to enjoy him. We need never pause to inquire whether we've crossed a line or become overindulgent. You need never fear feeling too good about God.

That's not to say our *sensual* appetites should be left

27

unchecked. The Bible is full of prohibitions and restrictions on how and to what extent we indulge our fleshly and bodily desires. But no such rules exist for our *spiritual* appetites.

Many think of religion in general and Christianity in particular as a sour and depressing attempt to suppress human desire and deprive us of the delights of life. Nothing could be further from the truth! *Christianity forbids us no pleasures, save those that lead to temporal misery and eternal woe.* Please read that again. God has forbidden you *nothing* that is conducive to your ultimate satisfaction and delight. Nothing!

So, I'll say it again. You cannot desire pleasure too much. You *can* desire the *wrong kind* of pleasure. You can rely on the wrong things to satisfy your soul, things that God has forbidden. But the intensity of the soul's search for joy cannot be too great or too deep or too sharp or too powerful. The divine invitation is that we would satisfy our voracious appetite for spiritual delight by indulging our souls in every delicacy that God has to offer. He bids us imbibe the waters of spiritual refreshment from a well that never runs dry. He points us to the river of his delights (Ps. 36:8) and says: 'Drink!' We are urged to immerse and soak and saturate ourselves in the spiritual pleasures and blessings that he lavishly and abundantly and happily pours forth through Jesus and the power of the Holy Spirit.

No, this is not sin! Sin is the misguided and selfish determination to seek happiness in places where ultimately only emptiness and disillusionment are found. Spiritual hunger is not sin. Sin is declining God's offer of a filet mignon to fill our spiritual bellies with rancid ground beef.

Often when I share this vision of the Christian life, people accuse me of being a closet liberal or a humanist or a self-indulgent egotist. They don't understand how it can be 'Christian' to argue that our pre-eminent goal in life should be the pursuit of pleasure . . . in God. The idea strikes them as selfish, as inconsistent with self-sacrifice and obedience. What I'm recommending seems terribly out of sync with the reality of pain and hardship and frustration and disappointment that we all face. Worst of all, they believe it is contrary to the biblical call that we do everything for the glory of God. It seems so 'me-centered', when the Bible demands that we be 'God-centered'.

I've almost come to expect having 2 Timothy 3:4 thrown in my face, as if I'm a culprit in contributing to the decadence of 'the last days' (2 Tim. 3:1). After all, doesn't Paul warn us about people who are 'lovers of pleasure rather than lovers of God' (2 Tim. 3:4)? Yes, and we ought to be leery of them, but I plead not guilty!

The key words in this verse are 'rather than', for they highlight options that are mutually exclusive. The 'pleasure' that people love, and Paul condemns, is sensual, self-indulgent satisfaction that shuts God out. The 'pleasure' that I have in mind, and Paul approves, is precisely pleasure in God as God. *He* is our exceeding great reward. *He* is the treasure (and pleasure) we seek. Christian Hedonism deplores any pursuit of pleasure that does not have God as the foundation and focus of its enjoyment.

Paul rightly denounces lovers of pleasure without God. Christian Hedonism rightly applauds lovers of pleasure *in* God. To be a 'lover of God' rather than 'pleasure' is to find in him, not it, the satisfaction our souls so desperately crave. God is loved when he is the rock on which we stand, the shelter in whom we seek refuge, the oasis where we find refreshment. 2 Timothy 3:4, therefore, is not a problem for Christian Hedonism but a prooftext!

What people fail to see, and what I hope to make clear in this book, is that pursuing the gladness of your heart and pursuing the glory of God are not separate, but one and the same endeavor. *God's greatest glory is in your gladness in him.*

Why Self-Denial is a Hedonistic Choice

There is one other biblical text that many believe undermines Christian Hedonism. The words of Jesus in Mark 8:34-37 may strike you as a threat to the validity of everything I've said to this point:

> *If anyone would come after me, let him deny himself and take up his cross and follow me. For whoever would save his life will lose it, but whoever loses his life for my sake and the gospel's will save it. For what does it profit a man to gain the whole world and forfeit his life? For what can a man give in return for his life?*

Doesn't this dilute, if not destroy, my emphasis on the pursuit of one's pleasure, even if that pleasure is in God? I don't think so. In fact, it encourages your pursuit of pleasure! Let me explain what I think Jesus is saying.

When he calls on you to deny your 'self' he doesn't mean that you should give up all concern for the state of your soul. Jesus isn't advocating the suppression of personal desire or recommending that you dress shabbily or skip meals or neglect personal hygiene. Jesus is actually appealing to the concern you have for yourself and the eternal welfare of your soul. The only way you can respond appropriately to his call for 'self' denial is if you are wholeheartedly committed to the happiness and eternal welfare of your 'self'. I know this sounds paradoxical, if not downright contradictory, so let me explain what I think he had in mind.

Imagine what your response would be to these words of Jesus if you were convinced that concern for your own soul was sinful or selfish. You would forfeit all incentive for obeying him! The only reason it makes sense to heed his exhortation is because of intense, personal, passionate concern for what might happen to you if you don't. Jesus calls on us to deny ourselves because otherwise we'll die! We must 'lose' our lives if we hope to 'save' them. And it is the legitimacy of that personal hope on which Jesus bases his appeal. Clearly, Jesus grounds his exhortation in the inescapable reality of human desire for one's own welfare and happiness and well-being. Here's how C. S. Lewis explains it:

> The New Testament has lots to say about self-denial, but not about self-denial as an end in itself. We are told to deny ourselves and to take up our crosses in order that we may follow Christ; and nearly every description of what we shall ultimately find if we do so contains an appeal to desire.[1]

Jesus is aware that we desire what is best for ourselves. He neither rebukes us for it nor calls for repentance as if it were sinful. In fact, he intentionally targets that universal desire and entreats us based upon its undeniable presence in our souls. His somewhat paradoxical advice is that the best thing you can do for your 'self' is to deny 'self'! Eternal life is the best and most advantageous thing you can obtain for your 'self', but it may cost you temporal life and the passing pleasures of sinful self-indulgence.

What possible profit is there from enhancing your physical life now if it costs you eternal life in the age to come? Self-denial, John Piper reminds us, 'has value precisely in proportion to the superiority of the reality embraced above the one desired. Self-denial that is not based on a desire for some superior goal will become the ground of boasting.'[2]

Jesus is simply asking that you sacrifice the lesser blessings of temporal and earthly comforts in order to gain the greater blessings of eternal and unending pleasure. Do what is best for your 'self', says Jesus, and deny your 'self'! To refuse to follow Jesus is to deny your 'self' the greatest imaginable joy. His call is for us to renounce our vain attempt to satisfy our souls through illicit sex and ambition and earthly fortune. Instead, do yourself a favor: follow Jesus and gain true life, true joy, true pleasure.

Jesus is not telling us to ignore our needs or to repress our longings but to fulfill them ... in him! Consider the now well-known words of C. S. Lewis:

> If there lurks in most modern minds the notion that to desire our own good and earnestly to hope for the enjoyment of it is a bad thing, I submit that this notion has crept in from Kant and the Stoics and is no part of the Christian faith. Indeed, if we consider the unblushing promises of reward and the staggering nature of the rewards promised in the Gospels, it would seem that Our Lord finds our desires not too strong, but too weak. We are half-hearted creatures, fooling about with drink and sex and ambition when infinite joy is offered [to] us, like an ignorant child who wants to go on making mud pies in a slum because he cannot imagine what is meant by the offer of a holiday at the sea. We are far too easily pleased.[3]

Microscopes, Telescopes, and the Glory of God

I want to return to my earlier statement that *God's greatest glory is in your passionate gladness in him*. Perhaps an analogy will help illustrate what this means.

Consider the difference between a *microscope* and a *telescope* and how it relates to our knowledge and enjoyment of God, and what it means to *glorify* him.[4] Both a microscope and a telescope are designed to *magnify* objects. So, too, are we. The Bible repeatedly calls on us, especially in the Psalms, to magnify the Lord: 'Oh, *magnify* the LORD with me, and let us exalt his name together' (Ps. 34:3; cf. 35:27). 'I will praise the name of God with a song; I will *magnify* him with thanksgiving' (Ps. 69:30). 'My soul *magnifies* the Lord, and my spirit rejoices in God my Savior' (Luke 1:46-47).

But there are two entirely different ways of magnifying God, one of which exalts him and the other which demeans him.

First, you can magnify God the way a microscope would. A microscope magnifies by focusing on something quite small, most often invisible to the naked eye, and causing it to look much, much bigger than it really is. This is magnification by distortion! This is *not* how we are to magnify God! Tragically, though, that's how many Christians think of God and how they are to worship him. They think that in their lives and in their prayers and in their praise they are causing God to look bigger and greater and more glorious than he really is, in and of himself.

Worship is not like blowing up a balloon. God is not honored by human inflation, as if the breath of our praise enhances and expands his visibility and worth. To think that apart from our praise God remains shrunken and shriveled is to dishonor him who 'gives to all mankind life and breath and everything' (Acts 17:25).

But you can also magnify God the way a telescope would. A telescope magnifies by focusing on something indescribably huge and massive and causing it to appear as it really and truly is. A telescope peers into the distant realms of our universe and displays before our eyes the massive, unfathomable, indescribable dimensions of what is there. Only in this latter sense are we called to *magnify* the Lord. Of course, the analogy breaks down, as all analogies eventually do, because God is infinitely greater than anything you can see through a telescope. Indeed, he created and fashioned everything you can see through a telescope. But I trust you get my point.

This is the point Paul makes in Ephesians 3:21 at the conclusion of his intercessory prayer on behalf of the Ephesian church (Eph. 3:14-19):

Now to him who is able to do far more abundantly than all that we ask or think, according to the power at work within us, to him be glory in the church and in Christ Jesus throughout all generations, forever and ever. Amen (Eph. 3:20-21; emphasis mine).

In other words, 'May God be magnified!' May God be joyfully seen for who he truly is (and not for what we've made him to be), and because of what he has done, in all of his majesty and splendor and glory!

Getting a Grip on Glory

I've used the word 'glory' several times so far. It's a good biblical term, but perhaps it would help if I defined what I mean. I simply define glory as *the beauty of God unveiled*. Glory is the resplendent radiance of his power and his personality. Glory is all of God that makes God God, and shows him to be worthy of our praise and our boasting and our trust and our hope and our confidence and our joy.

Glory is the external elegance of the internal excellencies of God. Glory is what you see and experience and feel when God goes public with his beauty!

The ultimate reason God sustained you through the night and awakened you this morning and mercifully preserves your soul even now is so his name might be exalted. This is the same reason your car didn't crash on the way to the store or church where you purchased this book. It's why your heart continues to beat and blood rushes through your veins and your lungs continue to inflate. God's own glory is what he aims for in all he does. That is why God's glory must be what *we* aim for in all we do.

Let me change words for a moment and put in place of 'magnify' and 'glorify' the word 'exalt'. Paul could just as easily have written: 'Let him be *exalted* in the church and in Christ Jesus to all generations.' None of us will disagree with that. But where we differ is how best to do it. What is the most biblical and effective way to *exalt* God? How might we engage in the *exaltation* of the Creator? The answer is in another word, the spelling of which differs in only one letter from our first word: *exultation*. This is *not* semantic nitpicking. The Christian life hangs suspended on it!

To exult is to rejoice and to celebrate. We exult when we find deep satisfaction in an individual or experience. Whether we say it, shout it, or merely sigh with a profound sense of delight, there is fascination and joy and gladness of heart. There is an emotionally explosive dimension to exultation: Wow! Whoopee! Unbelievable! Man! Oh, yeah! Or as my daughter would say: Sweet! To exult in something or someone is to find in them happiness, gladness, joy, complete and utter satisfaction; it is to savor them.

I believe that exulting in God is the most biblical and effective means for exalting him! Or to put it in other terms: *God is praised when he is prized!* Understanding God is but a means to enjoying God. We tell others of this glory so that we might raise joy in ourselves and in them at what we have told.

How do you measure the value of something you hold dear? How do you assess the worth of a prize? Is it not by the depth of delight it induces in your heart? Is it not by the intensity and quality of your joy in what it is? Is it not by how excited and enthralled and thrilled you are in the manifold display of its attributes, characteristics, and properties? Is it not by the extent of the sacrifice you are willing to make to gain it, to guard it, and to keep it? In other words, your satisfaction in what the treasure is and does for you is the standard or gauge by which its glory (worth and value) is revealed. The treasure, which is God, is most glorified in and by you when your pleasure in him is maximal and optimal.

That is why if you want to *elevate* God, *celebrate* God! Treasure him. Prize him. Delight in him. Enjoy him. In doing so you *magnify* him, you show him to be the most wonderful and sweet and all-sufficient being in the universe.

This book is an invitation to glorify God by relishing him now and forever. Enjoying God is not a momentary diversion from more important responsibilities you have as a Christian. Enjoying God is not a means to a higher end. This *is* the end. Enjoying is not a pathway to the pinnacle. It is the pinnacle, the purpose for which you and I live. As such, it is the solution to our struggle with sin. The antidote to apathy is the enjoyment of God. It is the divine catalyst for human change.

Practical Hints

I began this chapter with an idea unfamiliar to many evangelicals (and perhaps heretical to a few!). I suggested that when it comes to satisfying our spiritual appetites, *there is no such thing as excess*. I realize in saying this I'm swimming upstream against the swift and stubborn waters of years of religious tradition. People for whom the word 'restraint' summarizes their concept of Christianity will squirm at my words. But I'm persuaded from Scripture that God places no restraints on us, imposes no rules of temperance or laws requiring moderation or boundaries beyond which we cannot go in seeking to enjoy him.

So what might be done of a practical nature to avail ourselves of this incredible invitation? Permit me to close this chapter by appealing to Jonathan Edwards yet again. In an unpublished sermon on Song of Solomon 5:1,[5] he makes several suggestions that are worthy of our attention. I want to mention only three. As we've come to expect, Edwards had a unique way of expressing himself on such points.

A Focused Heart

First, we should 'endeavor to increase spiritual appetites by meditating on spiritual objects.'[6] Each time we surrender our minds to meditate on base and sordid objects their grip on our lives is intensified. To think we can decrease our affinity for sinful pleasure apart from a concentrated fixation on the spiritually sublime is simply delusional.

Paul said as much in his letter to the Philippians: 'Finally, brothers, whatever is true, whatever is honorable, whatever is just, whatever is pure, whatever is lovely, whatever is commendable, if there is any excellence, if there is anything worthy of praise, think about these things' (Phil. 4:8). Merely acknowledging that such 'things' exist is woefully deficient. More than defining them and defending them as worthy of our affection is needed. We must actually 'think' about them, ponder them, pore over them, and become vulnerable to the power God has invested in them to transform our values and feelings and to energize our volitions.

Perhaps no one was more diligent in meditating on spiritual objects than David, King of Israel. I'm reminded of two statements in particular, both of which express the intensity and exclusivity of his devotion. Both are found in my favorite psalm:

- *I say to the Lord, 'You are my Lord; I have no good apart from you' (Ps. 16:2; see also Ps. 73:25-26).*

- *I have set the Lord always before me; because he is at my right hand, I shall not be shaken (Ps. 16:8).*

I was helped greatly in my understanding of these texts by something Larry Crabb recently confessed. Larry's honesty is disarming and challenging. He's not afraid to admit what the rest of us skillfully hide. Following his brother's tragic death in an airplane crash, Larry found himself wrestling with God and trying to make sense of what seemed so senseless. In a moment of frightening candidness, he cried out to God: 'I know you are all I have, but I don't know you well enough for you to be all that I need.'[7]

What I hear Larry saying is that *the measure of our satisfaction is the degree to which we can both trust and rejoice when all we have left is God.* Neither Larry nor the psalmist is denying that other things are good or lack the capacity to please. But they please only when acknowledged and enjoyed as gifts of God without whom all else is ultimately meaningless. Everything without God is pathetically inferior to God without everything. Or as C. S. Lewis put it, 'he who has God and everything else has no more than he who has God only.'[8]

This is why David was so diligent to avert his eyes from all lesser beauty. His resolve was to set the Lord before him, to concentrate his attention and the energies of his soul on the majesty and power of the One who alone would sustain him when all else is shaking. This was not an infrequent or occasional choice or one to which he reverted only in times of crisis, but an orientation of life to which he was 'always' committed. We would do well to follow his example.

During the revival known as the First Great Awakening in New England (1740-42), Edwards' own wife and mother of their eleven children, Sarah, experienced something similar to what David describes. Her testimony is a stunning example of the life-changing, sin-defeating power of what happens when the beauty of God is seen and known and felt. Consider these few short excerpts from her testimony.[9]

She speaks of 'a delightful sense of the immediate presence and love of God' that *was so near and so real that I seemed scarcely conscious of anything else*' (emphasis mine). This is not the cognitive affirmation of divine omnipresence but the experiential exhilaration of God's palpable nearness. More than an intellectual awareness of God's presence, this 'delightful sense' of his immanence became a dominant, sin-killing force in her life. The intensity of it dulled her awareness of 'anything else' and diminished her capacity to yield to the promptings of the flesh.

Sarah felt a happiness that lifted her 'above earth and hell, out of the reach of everything here below', so that she could look 'on all the rage and enmity of men or devils with a kind of holy indifference and an undisturbed tranquility'. She felt herself 'more perfectly weaned from all things here below than ever before. The whole world, with all its enjoyments and all its troubles seemed to be nothing:—My God was my all, my only portion.'

'I was,' she said, 'entirely swallowed up in God, as my only portion, and His honour and glory was the object of my supreme desire and delight.' She particularly recalls one encounter with God's love that 'was worth more than all the outward comfort and pleasure which I had enjoyed in my whole life put together. It was a pure delight which fed and satisfied the soul. It was *pleasure*, without the least sting or any interruption. It was a *sweetness* which my soul was lost in. It seemed to be all that my feeble frame could sustain, of that fulness of joy which is felt by those who behold the face of Christ and share His love in the heavenly world.'

The glorious knowledge of the beauty of Christ's love and his nearness to her soul proved more powerful and winsome than all the pleasures and outward comforts this present world could afford. 'The spiritual beauty of the Father and the Saviour seemed to engross my whole mind; and it was the instinctive feeling of my heart, "Thou art; and there is none beside Thee." I never felt such an entire emptiness of self-love or any regard to any private, selfish interest of my own. It seemed to me that I had entirely done with myself. I felt that the opinions of the world concerning me were nothing, and that I had no more to do with any outward interest of my own than with that of a person whom I never saw. The glory of God seemed to be all, and in all, and to swallow up every wish and desire of my heart.'

Some eight years later, Jonathan himself tasted a similar spiritual sweetness in the midst of the most bitter experience of his earthly life. After twenty-four years of faithful pastoral service to the church in Northampton, Massachusetts, he was unjustly fired by an overwhelming vote of the male membership. But like Sarah, he seemed to live 'above earth and hell, out of the reach of everything here below', so that he looked 'on all the rage and enmity of men or devils with a kind of holy indifference and an undisturbed tranquility.' How so? One church member sympathetic to Edwards described his reaction to being dismissed:

> That faithful witness received the shock, unshaken. I never saw the least symptoms of displeasure in his countenance the whole week, but he appeared like a man of God, whose happiness was out of the reach of his enemies and whose treasure was not only a future but a present good, overbalancing all imaginable ills of life, even to the astonishment of many who could not be at rest without his dismission.[10]

Postured for Passion

Edwards' second word of advice is that you should 'endeavor to promote spiritual appetites by laying yourself in the way of allurement.'[11] Posture your life so that you may be easily enticed by the beauty of Christ. Make it easy on your soul by exposing your senses to those things that awaken spiritual desire and deepen holy longings.

God has appointed specific activities that are designed to ignite passion for his Son and elicit insatiable hunger for his presence. Certainly we don't need to be told yet again of the role of prayer and Scripture, but perhaps another reminder of the role of the eucharist is in order. Edwards himself said this about the blessed sacrament:

> *We ought carefully and with the utmost seriousness and consideration attend* the sacrament of the Lord's Supper: this was appointed for this end, to draw forth longings of our souls toward Jesus Christ. *Here are the glorious objects of spiritual desire by visible signs represented to our view. We have Christ evidently set forth crucified. . . . Here we have that spiritual meat and drink represented and offered to excite our hunger and thirst; here we have all that spiritual feast represented which God has provided for poor souls; and here we may hope in some measure to have our longing souls satisfied in this world by the gracious communications of the Spirit of God.*[12]

My family and I attend a church that practices weekly communion. I thought I had a good grasp of its meaning and approached it with sufficient reverence. But Edwards' words are a challenge to me. If he's right, and I think he is, the bread and wine exist not simply to stir cognitive remembrance but to light a fire of unquenchable longing for the Savior whose body and blood they symbolize. These visible signs are also a means of grace by which the Spirit excites and intensifies our thirst for what Jesus alone can offer. So come to the eucharist hungry and feast on the Son of God.

The Way of Worship

Third, 'we should express our longings to God; they will increase by being expressed.'[13] Passions often wither in silence. Undeclared delight is a virtual contradiction in terms. God never intended for our joy to be quiescent. 'I think we delight to praise what we enjoy,' said Lewis, 'because *the praise not merely expresses but completes the enjoyment; it is its appointed consummation* (emphasis mine).'[14]

There's nothing more frustrating than an experience of sheer delight in the absence of someone with whom you can share it. As an avid baseball fan few things get my juices flowing like a successful double-steal or hit-and-run or, better still, a grand-slam in the bottom of the ninth inning. My instinctive reaction is to shout at anyone within earshot: 'Did you see that? Wow!' To leave my exultation unexpressed is unthinkable. Although I enjoy watching a new film in an unoccupied theater (it's a little strange, I know), I invariably rush home to tell my wife how great it was (or how pathetic, as the case may be).

So it is with worship, but on an even grander scale. To grasp what this really means 'we must suppose ourselves to be in perfect love with God—drunk with, drowned in, dissolved by, that delight which, far from remaining pent up within ourselves as incommunicable, hence hardly tolerable, bliss, flows out from us incessantly again in effortless and perfect expression, our joy is no more separable from the praise in which it liberates and utters itself than the brightness a mirror receives is separable from the brightness it sheds.'[15]

Worship is not only the expression of joy, it is the soil in which additional and even greater joy is seeded. As we celebrate God in word and praise, the Spirit works within to cultivate still deeper delight in God that cries out to be vented in exuberant exultation. Enjoyment issues in worship. Worship incites knowledge. Knowledge awakens joy. This joy issues in worship ... and so it goes, to the gladness of our hearts and the glory of God!

---

[1] C. S. Lewis, 'The Weight of Glory,' in *The Weight of Glory and Other Addresses*, edited and with an introduction by Walter Hooper (New York: Simon & Schuster, 1996), p. 25.

[2] John Piper, *Desiring God* (Sisters, OR: Multnomah Books, 1996), p. 244.

[3] Lewis, 'The Weight of Glory,' pp. 25-26 (emphasis mine).

[4] The idea for this illustration comes from Piper, *The Dangerous Duty of Delight* (Sisters, OR: Multnomah Publishers, 2001), p. 17.

[5] Jonathan Edwards, 'Sacrament Sermon on Canticles 5:1' (circa 1729). Edited version with introduction by Kenneth P. Minkema.

[6] Ibid., p. 14.

[7] Larry Crabb, 'Fly on the Wall: A Conversation About Authentic Transformation Among Dallas Willard, Larry Crabb, & John Ortberg,' in *Conversations: A Forum for Authentic Transformation*, Volume 1 (Spring 2003), p. 30.

[8] C. S. Lewis, 'The Weight of Glory,' in *The Weight of Glory and Other Addresses*, edited and with an introduction by Walter Hooper (New York: Simon & Schuster, 1996), p. 31.

[9] These excerpts are taken from the complete text as it is found in *The Works of Jonathan Edwards*, Vol. I (Edinburgh:

The Banner of Truth Trust, 1979 [1834]), pp. lxii-lxx.

[10] Quoted in Iain Murray, *Jonathan Edwards: A New Biography* (Edinburgh: Banner of Truth Trust, 1987), p. 327 (emphasis mine).

[11] Edwards, 'Sacrament Sermon on Canticles 5:1,' p. 14.

[12] Ibid., pp. 14-15. Emphasis mine.

[13] Ibid., p. 15.

[14] C. S. Lewis, 'A Word About Praising,' in *Reflections on the Psalms* (New York: Harcourt, Brace and World, 1958), p. 95.

[15] Ibid., p. 96.

Chapter Three
The Power of Beauty

For me, a picture should be something likeable, joyous, and beautiful—yes, beautiful. There are enough ugly things in life for us not to add to them.

Pierre Auguste Renoir

What is it about God that makes him so *enjoyable?* Is there something about God that makes our pursuit of him a worthwhile endeavor? What is it about God that is so *fascinating?* There has to be a reason for arguing that he *excites* and *captivates* and *satisfies* the human heart in a way that nothing else can. Why do we believe we should turn from all worldly allurements and diversions to focus on knowing and seeing and experiencing the triune God of the Bible? What is it about him that when known and seen and experienced empowers the human soul to feel sickened in the presence of sin and satisfied in the divine embrace?

I've spoken several times of rejoicing at the 'glory' and 'perfection' and 'excellency' of God and relishing in the beauty of Christ as the very reason for our existence. What might we know or see of this glory and these perfections that should evoke such a response? There must be something about God's excellency that makes it an experience worthy of overcoming all obstacles and making every sacrifice to obtain. To encourage you to pursue pleasure in Jesus makes no sense unless you have good reason to believe there is something about him more pleasing than what the world, flesh, and the devil have to offer.

One Thing

The answer to our question(s) is found in the unitary, single-minded resolve of King David. 'One thing have I asked of the LORD, that will I seek after: that I may dwell in the house of the LORD all the days of my life, *to gaze upon the beauty of the Lord and to inquire in his temple*' (Ps. 27:4; emphasis mine). He makes his point yet again in Psalm 145:5, declaring: 'On the glorious splendor of your majesty, and on your wondrous works, I will meditate.' The answer to our question, the object of David's pursuit, is the incomparable, transcendent, all-satisfying, sublime *beauty* of God.

David's resolution reminds me of a scene in the movie *City Slickers*. Curly, a grizzled, old cowboy, played by Jack Palance, pokes a bony finger in the air and tells city slicker Billy Crystal that the meaning of life is found in 'this, just one thing'. When Crystal looks bemusedly at his own finger and asks what the 'one thing' is, Curly says that it's something he has to find out for himself. It's different for every person. But if you are a Christian, it's the same thing for all of us. Our 'one thing' is the glory of God.

David didn't lead an easy life. Being King of Israel wasn't all it was cracked up to be. David didn't make it any easier with his adulterous relationship with Bathsheba and the shattering consequences it brought on him and the nation as a whole. That is why David's resolution is so stunning.

In view of David's circumstances, one might have excused him had he opted for a little peace and quiet, or perhaps a permanent and safe home away from his enemies, or at least a month's paid vacation! With all the struggles he faced and the heartache he endured, most of us would be willing to cut the King a little slack.

One need only read verses 1-3 of psalm 27 to get a sense for what David faced on a daily basis. He speaks of 'evildoers' who 'assail' him (v. 2). Their ravenous desire is to 'eat up' his flesh (v. 2), a vivid metaphor of their murderous intent. He speaks of 'adversaries and foes' (v. 2) who sought every opportunity to destroy his reputation. He envisions an 'army' (v. 3) of enemies encamped around him and 'war' (v. 3) rising up to put an end to all he had worked to achieve. You would suppose David would think about what others were thinking (or plotting) about him.

But David couldn't get God off his mind! He aspired to only one thing: to *dwell* ... to *behold* ... to *meditate*. And who or what is the focus of this passion? Who or what had the capacity to elicit such dedication from a man who had every reason, humanly speaking, to look elsewhere for comfort and relief? The answer is God in all his uncreated beauty, his indescribable splendor, his glorious majesty, his unfathomable, ultimately incomprehensible grandeur.

David's identity wasn't wrapped up in his calling as king. He didn't wake up each day with a political agenda on his mind or a scheme for expanding the boundaries of his empire. David thought of one thing: to find a way to break free of routine entanglements that he might dwell in the presence of God; to avoid trivial activities that might divert his eyes from beholding God; to clear his mind of extraneous details that he might meditate upon the beauty and splendor of God; to set aside less important tasks that he might bask in the invigorating light and glory of everything that makes God an object of our affection and delight and adoration.

Aesthetic Joy

As I write these words and you read them we are together experiencing a small part of what it means to be created in the image of God. But there is more to the divine image than simply the capacity to think. God is also a volitional being who deliberates and chooses. He is a moral being who burns with holy anger against unrighteousness and rejoices in the good. He is a self-reflective God who contemplates his own existence and the eternal purpose he is pursuing in Christ. As image-bearers, we reflect these capacities in our experience as well.

An often-overlooked dimension in who we are as created in God's image is our capacity both to recognize and rejoice in beauty as well as feel revulsion at what is ugly or deformed. In other words, we are inescapably *aesthetic*. We've been hardwired both to discern the presence of beauty in God and his creation and to delight in it. God is himself the consummate artist whose creativity transcends our wildest imagination. We share in this divine capacity both to create (in a secondary and derivative sense) and celebrate beauty. Sin has distorted, but not destroyed, this facility in our souls.

The reality of the aesthetic dimension in my soul was awakened from slumber when I first encountered the French impressionist Pierre Auguste Renoir (1841-1919). The Phillips Collection of art, permanently housed in Washington, D.C., was on temporary loan in Dallas, Texas. I had the incredible privilege of seeing what I believe to be his greatest artistic work: *The Luncheon of the Boating Party*. I was aesthetically naïve at the time, not knowing what, if anything, I was supposed to do or say. So I didn't do or say anything! I honestly felt incapable of meaningful action or speech. I was caught completely off guard, engulfed by a new and unfamiliar sensation. It was overwhelming and breathtaking. I lost track of time and had to be retrieved by my wife who insisted that we move on; after all, other people were waiting their turn. But it kept drawing me in.

Only those who've had a similar experience, whether with Renoir or some other artistic embodiment of beauty, know what it's like. For me, I was mesmerized by its color, brilliance, proportion, and life. The image evoked within me an entirely new and unfamiliar sense of wonder and joy. Philosophers call it aesthetic contemplation or *disinterested delight*. The latter phrase almost sounds like a contradiction in terms. If you 'delight' in something you can hardly lack interest in it! What I mean is that I felt no inclination to ask of Renoir or his work how I might benefit from it or to what use it might be put to satisfy some ulterior desire. My joy and delight in the painting didn't have an 'in order that' appended to it, as if it existed to help me achieve some higher or more ultimate goal. It was just there, to be admired, marveled at, and enjoyed.

To this day I remain an unashamed devotee of Renoir and have numerous prints of his greatest works on my office wall at home. I just noticed I'm also drinking coffee from a mug on which is found his painting, *Two Sisters on the Terrace* (the original is housed in The Art Institute of Chicago).

My encounter with Renoir brought me into touch with the presence in my soul of a clamoring, incessant desire for unending beauty. I was awakened in a fresh way to the role of wonder, awe, and amazement in life, and the power of the aesthetic dimension to transform the human heart. I'm not alone in this. Beauty has a universal reach. No human is immune from the magnetic appeal of whatever he/she regards as beautiful. In *The Brothers Karamazov*, Fyodor Dostoyevski placed on the lips of one of his characters the observation that 'beauty is the battlefield where God and Satan contend with each other for the hearts of men'.[1] The one, God, is supreme glory and splendor. The other, Satan, is supreme ugliness and perversion.

Someone once said, 'I can't define "obscenity", but I know it when I see it!' The point is that there is often an intuitive recognition of what we otherwise struggle to put into words. We don't always know how to articulate the concept but we instinctively feel its power in our hearts. If the ugliness of obscenity is whatever evokes revulsion and moral disdain, perhaps we could define beauty as whatever stirs delight and moral approval.

Beauty is shrouded in mystery. We can't easily explain why something is beautiful, why it captivates and tantalizes. We are simply drawn by it. We are entranced. It touches something deep in the soul that we can't express or put our finger on. It stirs thoughts and emotions and passions and desires and joys that can't be expounded. Beauty has the strange capacity to arouse the soul in a way that little else can. The experience of it is lucid testimony to our having been fashioned in the likeness of a God who himself embodies quintessential aesthetic glory.

Is Beauty in the Eye of the Beholder?

Let's return for a moment to Renoir. Is there something intrinsic to *The Luncheon of the Boating Party* that warrants predicating beauty of it? Is its beauty an objective property, always present irrespective of the opinion of people like you and me? Or is this painting beautiful because I regard it as such? Would beauty still be an appropriate word should someone else regard this painting as banal or unimaginative (pity the soul who thinks it such!)?

I'm asking whether beauty is in things, be it a painting, a sunset, a garden of flowers, irrespective of human opinion, or does human opinion create beauty by attributing to things the power to please? Do things evoke pleasure because they are beautiful, or is beauty the pleasure that things evoke? Philosophers refer to the former as *objectivism* and the latter as *subjectivism*.

The fact that people disagree both about the criteria of beauty and whether ascriptions of beauty ought to be made is often used as an argument against objectivism. But aesthetics is not like mathematics. Aesthetic qualities are more subtle and elusive and more difficult to describe than scientific formulae.

People from the area may think me odd for saying this, but one of the most beautiful places in the world is the Flint Hills just north of Wichita, Kansas, on Interstate 35. During the seven years I lived in Kansas City, Missouri, I made frequent trips to Oklahoma to visit family and friends. But I never dreaded the six-hour journey, knowing that a delectable visual feast awaited me on the road. I can't explain why it affects me the way it does, but I'm often left breathless by the splendor of those rolling meadows under a setting summer sun. It's as though I've been granted a brief glimpse of the splendor of what the New Earth will be in the ages to come.

Other visual properties, whether hue or structural harmony or brilliance, have the power to evoke in our hearts an intuitive delight. People often apply the word 'beauty' to audible properties such as melody, pitch, rhythm, harmony, and resolution. Bach's Brandenburg Concertos immediately come to mind. There is also a sense in which the concept of beauty evokes thoughts of a sweet, pleasing aroma. The scent of a flower. The fragrance of perfume. The aroma of incense. Although less common, I've heard chefs and connoisseurs of fine food predicate beauty of the flavor of their favorite entrée or perhaps a perfectly aged wine.

Might we speak of certain *intellectual* properties or theorems or ideas as beautiful? The 2002 academy award for best picture was given to the Ron Howard film, *A Beautiful Mind*, and rightly so in my opinion. I see no reason to restrict beauty to merely physical properties of inanimate objects. Some predicate beauty of whatever soothes the soul or challenges the imagination or stretches our powers of perception or stirs the depths of our senses. Mathematical formulas and scientific theories and the narrative flow of a John LeCarre novel might all embody characteristics that we call beautiful.

I made an attempt in an earlier book to define beauty as 'whatever stuns and surprises and takes our breath away, whether the golden glow of a lingering sunset, the cavernous depths of the Grand Canyon, or the inaugural steps of a first-born child. Beauty is whatever causes our hearts to beat with increasing rapidity and sends chills down our spines or causes goose bumps to rise on our arms. Beauty is whatever stirs up worth in the human spirit and enables us to feel the dignity of self and the hope of tomorrow.'[2]

I don't hesitate to predicate beauty of human compassion or generosity or the dedication of a missionary that may well lead to martyrdom. Moral excellence can be as beautiful as Niagara Falls. Marital fidelity can be as elegant as the expanse of the Pacific Ocean. Is it not a 'beautiful' thing when justice prevails in our world (infrequent though it be), or when truth is vindicated or moral valor rewarded? Beauty is whenever what ought to be, is. TV news broadcasters often warn us in advance of 'an ugly scene' in the inner city where gang warfare has escalated or a domestic disturbance has disrupted a neighborhood. All this points to what we sense in our spirit, that beauty is found in racial harmony and peace and calm and reconciliation and reciprocity and compassion. Ugliness is the distortion of moral order and the violation of basic principles of right and wrong.

But what of God? Might we speak of him as beautiful?

The Beauty of God

You will search in vain in most theology books for a section on divine beauty. The idea is typically omitted from the traditional list of divine attributes. Most concede that God is, at minimum, the cause or source or origin of beauty. But Augustine rightly insisted that God is beauty itself, referring to him as 'my Father, supremely good, beauty of all things beautiful'.[3]

My initial response to the beauty of that Renoir masterpiece some twenty years ago was important because it stirred in me the realization that God desires no less, and indeed far more, from all of us in our relationship with him. God's revelatory manifestation of himself in creation, in providence, in Scripture, and pre-eminently in the face of his Son, Jesus Christ, is designed to evoke within the breathtaking delight and incomparable joy of which God alone is worthy. Beauty is that in God which makes him eminently desirable and attractive and quickens in the soul a realization that it was made for a different world.

God has sovereignly pulled back the curtain on his glory. He has disclosed himself on the platform of both creation and redemption that we might stand awestruck in his presence, beholding the sweet symmetry of his attributes, pondering the unfathomable depths of his greatness, baffled by the wisdom of his deeds and the limitless extent of his goodness. This is his *beauty*.

Divine beauty is absolute, unqualified, and independent. All created reality, precisely because it is derivative of the Creator, is beautiful in a secondary sense and only to the degree that it reflects the excellencies of God and fulfills the purpose for which He has made it. Perfect order, harmony, magnitude, integrity, proportion, symmetry, and brilliance are found in God alone. There is in the personality and activity of God neither clash of color nor offensive sound. He is in every conceivable respect morally exquisite, spiritually sublime, and aesthetically elegant.

The Spirit of God communicates God's beauty to this world through creation, the latter a reflection of divine glory. But whatever beauty we see now is but a faint echo of the invisible archetype from which it came, a dim foretaste and anticipation of the beauty of the consummated and transfigured world of the age to come. A fourth-century church father, Gregory of Nyssa, put it this way:

> Hope always draws the soul from the beauty which is seen to what is beyond, always kindles the desire for the hidden through what is constantly perceived. Therefore the ardent lover of beauty, although receiving what is always visible as an image of what he desires, yet longs to be filled with the very stamp of the archetype. And the bold request which goes up the mountains of desire asks this: to enjoy the Beauty not in mirrors and reflections, but face to face.[4]

God never intended for me to worship Renoir or the work of his hands, but to see in and through the latter a glimpse of the glory that yet awaits me. C. S. Lewis reminds, dare I say warns, us that

> the books or the music [or paintings] in which we thought the beauty was located will betray us if we trust to them; it was not in them, it only came through them, and

what came through them was longing. These things – the
beauty, the memory of our own past – are good images of
what we really desire; but if they are mistaken for the thing
itself, they turn into dumb idols, breaking the hearts of
their worshippers. For they are not the thing itself; they are
only the scent of a flower we have not found, the echo of a
tune we have not heard, news from a country we have never
visited.[5]

The aesthetic experience of God, the encounter of the human
soul with divine beauty, is more than merely enjoyable, it is
profoundly transforming. There is within it the power to
persuade and to convince the inquiring mind of truth. This
may well be the Spirit's greatest catalyst for change. Paul alluded
to this in 2 Corinthians 3:18 when he said, 'We all, with unveiled
face, *beholding* the glory of the Lord, are *being changed* into
his likeness from one degree of glory to another.' The point is
that *what we see is what we be!* We do not simply behold beauty:
beauty takes hold of us and challenges the allegiance of our
hearts. Beauty calls us to reshape our lives and exposes the
shabbiness of our conduct. It awakens us to the reality of a
transcendent Being to whose likeness of beauty we are being
called and conformed by his gracious initiative. Beauty has the
power to dislodge from our hearts the grip of moral and spiritual
ugliness. The soul's engagement with beauty elicits love and forges
in us a new affection that no earthly power can overcome.

Beauty also rebukes by revealing to us the moral deformity
of those things we've embraced above Jesus and by exposing the
hideous reality beyond the deceptively attractive façade of
worldly amusements. We are deceived by the ugliness of sin
because we haven't gazed at the beauty of Christ. Distortion
and perversion and futility are fully seen only in the perfect

light of integrity and harmony and purpose which are revealed in Jesus.

The Beauty of Incarnate Deity

Being spiritually smitten by divine beauty isn't simply an experience of joy that satisfies, it also *sustains* the soul through the fire of trial and loss and persecution. Beauty not only evokes pleasure, it imparts perseverance. A day is coming, and for many Christians worldwide already is, when the judgments of God against an idolatrous and unbelieving world will test the loyalty and maturity of God's people. When our homes are looted and our property stolen and our bodies imprisoned, only a heart tantalized by divine splendor will stand firm. When Christians suffer imprisonment and torture and the pressure to yield, only the God-intoxicated heart will endure.

I've spent a lifetime studying the history of Christianity and its heroes, and few stand taller in my book than a short, fiery-tempered, theologically stubborn man named Athanasius. Many of you will not have heard of him, but he is a marvelous example of how one is energized to persevere by the greatness of divine glory. There is also a sense in which *you owe your eternal life to his love of incarnate beauty*. Let me briefly share with you his story.

It all begins with a slick and slender heretic named Arius who ministered in a church in North Africa way back in the early years of the fourth century A.D. Arius argued that, like you and me, there was a time when the Son of God didn't exist! He was created 'out of nothing' no less so than stars and seaweed and Caesar and Sam Storms. Arius was happy to call Jesus the 'Son of God' but only as an expression of courtesy because of his superior participation in the grace of God. Arius and his followers 'worshipped' the Son and prayed to him, but denied his eternal deity. He was excommunicated in 318 and later condemned by the synod of Antioch and the Council of Nicea in 325. His death occurred one day before he was to be reinstated in ministry. He was apparently stricken with agonizing stomach spasms and died as he sat on the toilet (I suppose you could have done without knowing that!).

But this story is not really about Arius, but the man who withstood seemingly insurmountable odds and repeated attempts on his life to defend the deity of Christ.

Athanasius was born in North Africa in approximately A.D. 300. He was the sort of man who evoked either effusive admiration or contempt. Robert Payne tells us that

> in the history of the early Church no one was ever so implacable, so urgent in his demands upon himself or so derisive of his enemies. There was something in him of the temper of the modern dogmatic revolutionary: nothing stopped him. The Emperor Julian called him 'hardly a man, only a little manikin'. Gregory Nazianzen said he was 'angelic in appearance, and still more angelic in mind'. In a sense both were speaking the truth.[6]

He was, writes Christopher Hall, 'a theological street fighter, courageous, cagy, and cunning'.[7]

Athanasius was largely responsible for the condemnation of Arius and the formation of the Nicene Creed that many of you recite in church to this day. Central to that creed is the affirmation of Christ's full deity. Athanasius's perseverance, both personally and theologically, has placed the church forever in his debt. 'It may not be much of an exaggeration,' notes Roger Olson, 'to say that all Christians have Athanasius to thank that the theology of Jehovah's Witnesses is not the "orthodoxy" of most of Christendom.'[8]

When the emperor Constantine pressured Athanasius to reinstate Arius, our hero refused and defied the emperor's decree! This led to the first of five exiles, a two-year sojourn in the farthest outpost of the Roman Empire. When the emperor died, his son Constantius restored Athanasius but demanded that he confess that Jesus was only 'similar' to or 'like' the Father, a suggestion Athanasius condemned as rank heresy. Off to exile yet again. On another occasion, having been restored to his church, the service was interrupted by Roman guards who burst in with the intent of arresting and killing him. With the help of his congregation, Athanasius was able to elude their grasp and spent six years in hiding with several desert monks. Athanasius died in 373, having spent the last seven years of his life in relative peace and quiet.

Athanasius was a man captivated by the glory and splendor of Christ's divinity. There can be no salvation, he insisted, unless our savior be God. With Paul the apostle, Athanasius championed the truth that in Christ Jesus 'the whole fullness of deity dwells bodily' (Col. 2:9), and in him 'are hidden all the treasures of wisdom and knowledge' (Col. 2:3). For Athanasius to have quit would have been easy. Who could have blamed him had he yielded the battle to others and retreated to relative calm? Yet his heart had been touched by the splendor of incarnate Deity. He had tasted the sweetness of a Savior whose divine nature was worth dying to defend. His otherwise weak and self-protective soul was energized and sustained by the biblical portrait of the majesty and beauty of the eternal Son of God in the weakness of human flesh. One statement will disclose the secret to his persistent devotion. The achievements of our Savior, he wrote,

> resulting from his becoming man, are of such kind and number, that if one should wish to enumerate them, he may be compared to men who gaze at the expanse of the

sea and wish to count its waves.... [His achievements] all
alike are marvelous, and wherever a man turns his glance, he
may behold on that side the divinity of the Word, and be
struck with exceeding great awe![9]

Swallowed up in God

How do we behold this beauty? Where did Athanasius see
it? We encounter the beauty of the Lord when we spiritually
ingest the statements of Scripture concerning the wonders of
who God is and all he does. When we take the scintillating
truths of God and hide them in our hearts, meditate on them,
muse on them, soak our souls in them, so to speak, we become
infatuated with the exquisite personality of God. Let me close
this chapter with one example of how this may be done.

I love the doxological outbursts in Paul's letters, and none is
more poignant than I Timothy 1:17, where we read: 'To the
King of ages, immortal, invisible, the only God, be honor and
glory forever and ever. Amen.' I can't help but sense that they
explode from his heart like volcanic eruptions of incomparable
delight in God. In this short but staggering declaration of praise,
Paul answers five questions. *Who* is this God whom he so lavishly
praises? He is the *King*. *What* can be said about him? What
kind of King is he? He is *eternal, immortal, invisible,* indeed,
he is the *only God* there is. *How* are we to respond to him?
How do we worship him? We respond by ascribing to him *honor*
and *glory*. *When* or for how long do we worship him? *Forever*
and ever. And *why* should we do so? The answer to this final
question is found in verses 12-16 which precede.

Who is he? He is the *King*! He is certainly not a mere peas-
ant. Nor is he a prince or a pope or the president. He is the
King! This points to more than royalty. He is not merely regal
in his being. He is sovereign. The most important thing about a

King isn't that he is wealthy or majestic but that he *rules*. We often loudly proclaim the sovereign Kingship of God but just as often live as though it were not true. The fact is, as someone once said, 'People love God everywhere except on his throne!'

What kind of King is this? What are his attributes? What characterizes his being? Four things are mentioned here.

1. *He is eternal.* The Alpha and Omega. Without beginning. Without end. There are no term limits on his reign. He has always been King and he always will be King. There is no death that threatens the perpetuity of his sovereign authority. There is no usurping of power by a lesser rival to his throne. There are no coups, no revolutions (at least, none that succeed). There is no threat of impeachment. He is a King who rules eternally.

2. *He is immortal.* This King lives independently of all other life forms. He is the origin of all other life forms. His life is non-derivative. He does not live because of who anyone or anything else is or who or what anyone or anything else does. He simply *is*, irrespective and independent of all other *is*'s. His life is beyond the ravages of death, decay, or disintegration.

3. *He is invisible.* His being does not consist of material substance, which is created. As uncreated, he is pure spirit. No human eye can hope to 'see' him except to the degree that he chooses to reveal himself in some mediated form compatible with the finitude of man or in the incarnation of his Son. The glorious good news is that the invisible God became visible in the person of Jesus (John 1:18).

4. *He is the only God.*[10] All others are pretenders, impostors. '"You are my witnesses," declares the LORD, "and my servant whom I have chosen, that you may know and believe me, and understand that I am he. *Before me no god was formed, nor shall there be any after me. I, I am the LORD; and besides me there is no savior"'* (Isa. 43:10-11). '*And there is no other god*

besides me, a righteous God and a Savior; there is none besides me. Turn to me and be saved, all the ends of the earth! For I am God and there is no other' (Isa. 45:21-22).

How should we respond to this God? How can we speak of him? We should ascribe to him *honor!* We should ascribe to him *glory!* Our aim is to *ascribe* to God these attributes. We do not supply him with honor and glory. We do not have any honor and glory in our possession that he supposedly lacks, thinking that somehow we are able to give him what he does not already have inherently and eternally. Our role, our joy, is to ascribe and declare and proclaim to and of him what he is and always will be.

When do we do this? Should we start now? Is there a time when such praise and ascription and adoration will cease and we'll move on to better and more pleasing and more productive things? Our praise is *forever and ever. Amen!*

And why is God worthy of such praise? Paul's personal answer to this question has already been stated in verses 12-16. God has taken this hell-deserving sinner and lavished mercy and saving grace upon him. So, too, with you and me!

Hear Jonathan Edwards' response to this doxology. By God's grace, may it be our own:

> The first thing that I remember that ever I found any thing of that sort of inward, sweet delight in God and divine things, that I have lived much in since, was on reading those words, I Tim. 1.17. 'Now unto the king eternal, immortal, invisible, the only wise God, be honor and glory for ever and ever, Amen.' As I read the words, there came into my soul, and was as it were diffused thro' it, a sense of the glory of the Divine Being; a new sense, quite different from any thing I ever experienced before. Never any words of scripture

seemed to me as these words did. I thought with myself, how excellent a being that was; and how happy I should be, if I might enjoy that God, and be wrapt up to God in Heaven, and be as it were swallowed up in Him. I kept saying, and as it were, singing over these words of scripture to myself; and went to prayer, to pray to God that I might enjoy him; and prayed in a manner quite different from what I used to do; with a new sort of affection.[11]

Oh, to be consumed by the God of heaven, and be, as it were, swallowed up in that transcendent beauty! We don't want merely to see beauty, although that's where we have to begin. We long for something more, something so sacred and intimate that we hesitate to speak its name. The yearning that burns within is 'to be united with the beauty we see, to pass into it, to receive it into ourselves, to bathe in it, to become part of it.'[12] But at present, lamented Lewis, 'we are on the outside of the world, the wrong side of the door. We discern the freshness and purity of morning, but they do not make us fresh and pure. We cannot mingle with the splendours we see. But all the leaves of the New Testament are rustling with the rumour that it will not always be so. Some day, God willing, we shall get in.'[13]

Even so, come Lord Jesus!

---

[1] Cited in Thomas Dubay, *The Evidential Power of Beauty* (San Francisco: Ignatius Press, 1999), p. 20.

[2] Sam Storms, *Pleasures Evermore: The Life-Changing Power of Enjoying God* (Colorado Springs: NavPress, 2000), p. 147.

[3] *The Confessions of St. Augustine*, translated with an introduction and notes by John K. Ryan (New York: Image Books, 1960), 3.6.

[4] Quoted in Patrick Sherry, *Spirit and Beauty: An Introduction to Theological Aesthetics*, 2nd edition (London: SCM Press, 2002), p. 56.

[5] C. S. Lewis, 'The Weight of Glory,' in *The Weight of Glory and Other Addresses*, edited and with an introduction by Walter Hooper (New York: Simon & Schuster, 1996), p. 29.

[6] Robert Payne, *The Fathers of the Eastern Church* (New York: Dorset Press, 1989), p. 67.

[7] Christopher A. Hall, *Reading Scripture with the Church Fathers* (Downers Grove: IVP, 1998), p. 57.

[8] Roger E. Olson, *The Story of Christian Theology* (Downers Grove: IVP, 1999), pp. 161-62.

[9] Athanasius, *On the Incarnation* (Willits, CA: Eastern Orthodox Books, n.d.), p. 84.

[10] The KJV has the additional adjective 'wise', most likely a scribal insertion derived from Romans 16:27.

[11] Jonathan Edwards, *Letters and Personal Writings*, edited by George S. Claghorn. The Works of Jonathan Edwards, volume 16 (New Haven: Yale University Press, 1998), pp. 792-93.

[12] Lewis, 'The Weight of Glory,' p. 37.

[13] Ibid.

Chapter Four
What Handel Saw

Wonder is the normal response to splendor.

Thomas Dubay

Everyone knows Handel's *Messiah*, especially its rousing 'Hallelujah Chorus'. But not everyone knows the events in the life of George Frederick Handel (1685-1759) that inspired him to compose it.

Although born in Germany, Handel spent most of his adult life in England and eventually was made a citizen of the British empire. His father was a physician and had hoped that his son would follow in his steps. But George's interest in music was simply too overwhelming. He proceeded to write over twenty oratorios, more than forty full operas, as well as numerous concertos, cantatas, anthems, and sonatas.

Handel's life, however, was anything but tranquil. He was notoriously hot-tempered, frequently engaging in fights with other musicians. He hit an especially low point in 1741 at the age of 57. He was hopelessly in debt and was suffering from severe depression. One day a young poet named Charles Jennens appeared unannounced at his door. He delivered to Handel a collection of biblical passages under the title of *A Sacred Oratorio*. Half-heartedly, Handel began to read the manuscript. As he did, the prophetic utterance of Isaiah concerning the coming of Messiah began to lift him from his depression and reverberated in his soul: 'Wonderful, Counsellor, the Mighty God, the Everlasting Father, the Prince of Peace!'

As if by divine compulsion, Handel began to compose. He remained in virtual seclusion for the next twenty-five days, often going without food lest he be interrupted from his work. At times he would leap into the air, waving his hands, and shout 'Hallelujah!' When it was done, he said: 'I think I did see all heaven before me, and the Great God Himself.' What he wrote we know as the *Messiah*. As one author put it, 'Considering the immensity of the work [it filled 260 pages of manuscript], and the short time involved, it will remain, perhaps forever, the greatest feat in the whole history of musical composition' (Sir Newman Flower).

The Messiah was first performed on 13 April 1742. The following year it was performed in London for the first time. As the choir began to sing the majestic and now world-famous 'Hallelujah Chorus,' King George II was so stirred that he rose to his feet. The audience spontaneously followed suit and remained standing until the chorus had ended. This response has been customary ever since.

This piece may well be the single most inspiring and spiritually charged chorus of praise and worship ever written. So what moved Handel to write it? What inspired him? What had he seen or heard or felt that led him to compose this hymn of praise? The *Messiah* as a whole and the 'Hallelujah Chorus' in particular were inspired by Handel's meditation on the exalted and majestic portrait of the beauty of God in Revelation 4 – 5.

This passage is a vision of the majesty of a sovereign God in complete control of his creation. From an earthly perspective, it might seem that the enemies of the kingdom of God are winning. Christians are being persecuted, imprisoned, and martyred. Tragedy and trial and turmoil are rampant and the Great Dragon (Satan), the Beast, and the False Prophet appear to have the upper hand. All hope of light at the end of the tunnel grows dim because the tunnel has no end. The tunnel is all there is. History simply has no purpose. Dreams of finally emerging out the other side are shattered: there is no other side!

But John's vision reveals that appearances can be deceiving! The course of history isn't determined by political intrigue or military might, but by God. What John discovered, what Handel also must have learned, is that there are two worlds or two dimensions of reality. One is earthly and visible, the other is heavenly and invisible. And remarkably, it is the latter which controls and determines the former. Or better still, it is God who is sovereign over both!

It's as if the Holy Spirit says to John (and to us): 'Listen to me. Things are not as they appear. I'm about to show you things as they really are. I'm about to take you into the throne room of God himself. Things aren't running amok. The devil hasn't won. Evil hasn't triumphed. Neither fate nor cruel chance governs the universe. He who was and is and is to come has everything well in hand.'

Creator!

The voice John hears is that of Jesus Christ (cf. 1:10-11). As John looks, he's confronted with a breathtaking, knee-knocking, heart-pounding, eye-popping vision of the triune God. He sees the Lord enthroned, encircled, and extolled. What follows in these two chapters of the Apocalypse stretches the imagination and tests our capacity to grasp the beauty of God. Resist the temptation to read these verses as you would a newspaper or novel or even the book of Romans. May I suggest that as you read each element in this vision that you pause, close your eyes, and envision the majesty and glory of the scene.

In John's vision the throne of God is, as it should be, at the *center* of all heavenly activity. The throne is the focus of a series of concentric circles made up first of a rainbow, then a circle of the four living creatures, then a circle of the twenty-four thrones upon which the twenty-four elders sit. According to Revelation 5:11 (and again in 7:11), a great host of angels also encircled the throne. Eventually all creation joins the worshipping throng (see 5:13).

In Revelation 4:3 we see God in a resplendent blaze of unapproachable light, the jewels refracting the glory and majesty of his luminous beauty. Here is where all worship begins: in the throne room of heaven where God reigns supreme! When we see God as he is, incomparably sublime and incontestably sovereign, we will praise him as we should in unison with the heavenly hosts. This is not a pathetic deity wringing his hands over a world catapulting into oblivion. He does not pace the floor of heaven with furrowed brow, riddled with anxiety over the outcome of human history. God reigns!

If asked to describe God, what terms would you employ? I fear that many Christians are so deficient in their knowledge and experience of God that they'd portray him as a formless, passionless, grey blob of abstract power. John's vision, on the other hand, is a virtual kaleidoscope of color and sound and sight and smell! John sees all the colors of the rainbow magnified!

The one on the throne has the appearance of *jasper*, an opaque stone that tends to be red but is also found in yellow, green, and grayish blue. It suggests the qualities of majesty and holiness and is used later in Revelation as an image for the overall appearance of the New Jerusalem, which manifests the glory of God (21:11), and is the material from which its walls are constructed (21:18), as well as the first of its twelve foundations (21:19).

The *sardius* (or *carnelian*) is a red stone, similar in appearance to a ruby. It evokes the image of both divine jealousy and righteous wrath, both the burning zeal of God for the fame of his name and his just and resolute response to those who would bring reproach upon it. The *rainbow* reminds us of the faithfulness of God when he first set this sign in the heavens as a pledge to Noah following the great flood. Also found in Ezekiel 1:28, the rainbow reminds us that God's wrath and judgment, perhaps symbolized by the sardius as well as described in the subsequent visions, are tempered by his mercy and his promise to Noah never again to totally destroy the earth. In Ezekiel the rainbow is explicitly said to portray the radiant appearance of God's glory. Here it emanates like an *emerald*, reminding us that our God is filled not only with jealous zeal but tender-hearted affection.

Of course, John is not saying that God *is* a jasper or a sardius, but that his appearance was *like* such precious stones. This is not photographic reproduction but symbolic imagery. He wants to stir our imaginations and inflame our hearts, not fill our minds with endless facts.

The atmosphere of this scene is bathed in mystery and awash in wonder. Worship without wonder is lifeless and boring. Many have lost their sense of awe and amazement when it comes to God. Having begun with the arrogant presumption of knowing about God all that one can, they reduce him to manageable terms and confine him to a tidy theological box, the dimensions of which conform to their predilections of what a god ought to be and do. That they've lost the capacity to *marvel* at the *majesty* of God comes as little surprise. Warren Wiersbe explains:

> *We must recognize the fact that true wonder is not a passing emotion or some kind of shallow excitement. It has depth to it. True wonder reaches right into your heart and mind and shakes you up. It not only has depth, it has value; it enriches your life. Wonder is not cheap amusement that brings a smile to your face. It is an encounter with reality – with God – that brings awe to your heart. You are overwhelmed with an emotion that is a mixture of gratitude, adoration, reverence, fear,—and love. You are not looking for explanations; you are lost in the wonder of God.[1]*

Our wonder in God's presence, however, is not borne of ignorance but of knowledge. We know something about the majesty of God and for that reason are lost in wonder, love and praise. We can't stand in awe of someone of whom we're ignorant. Our wonder deepens with each degree of understanding.

But is it *practical* to worship when the world is falling apart? John's life is at risk. Of all the apostles, he alone has survived. Who knows how much longer he has? In such a crisis, why would the Spirit escort John into heaven and point to the adoring and passionate praise of angels and odd creatures and saints? Because it's the only thing that makes sense! Worship is no flight from reality. Nothing is more real than what John sees and hears and senses around the throne of God.

Worship is eminently practical because adoring and affectionate praise is what restores our sense of ultimate value. It exposes the worthless and temporary and tawdry stuff of this world. Worship energizes the heart to seek satisfaction in Jesus alone. In worship we are reminded that this world is fleeting and unworthy of our heart's devotion. Worship connects our souls with the transcendent power of God and awakens in us appreciation for true beauty. It pulls back the veil of deception and exposes the ugliness of sin and Satan. Worship is a joyful rebuke of the world. When our hearts are riveted on Jesus everything else in life becomes so utterly unnecessary and we become far less demanding.

The one so gloriously enthroned is encircled by the adoring throng of his creation. The first group mentioned are the twenty-four elders. They wear white garments and golden crowns (4:4), prostrate themselves before God in worship (4:10; 5:14; 11:16; 19:4), and cast before him their golden crowns (4:10). They sing hymns of praise to God (4:11; 5:9–10; 11:17–18), holding harps and bowls full of incense that are said to represent the prayers of Christians (5:8).

Some see in them *an exalted angelic order*, like the cherubim and seraphim, while others think they are *exalted Old Testament believers*. King David organized the temple servants into twenty-four orders of priests (1 Chron. 24:3-19), twenty-four Levitical gatekeepers (26:17-19), and twenty-four orders of Levites commissioned to prophesy, give thanks, praise God, and sing to the accompaniment of harps and lyres and cymbals (25:6-31).

Another possibility is that they are *exalted New Testament saints*, in particular, individual Christians who have sealed their faith through martyrdom and are now glorified and participating in an exalted heavenly life. Thrones are sometimes used as a metaphor for the heavenly reward of the righteous. But if they are only New Testament saints, why the number twenty-four? Could this be a symbol for their continuous, twenty-four-hour worship, day and night?

I find it difficult not to see in the number 'twenty-four' a reference to the twelve tribes of Israel and the twelve apostles of the New Testament church (they are associated again in 21:12-

14). If so, the Elders may be *representatives of the entire community of the redeemed from both testaments.* But are they *human* or *angelic* representatives? Probably the latter insofar as they bring the prayers of the saints before God (5:8) and sing of the redeemed in the third person (5:9-10). Also, the fact that these twenty-four elders are distinguished from the redeemed multitude in 7:9-17 indicates they are *angelic representatives of all the people of God.*

Rest assured of one thing. If they are in fact angels I doubt they look anything like the fat little cherubs with dimpled cheeks that hang playfully suspended above a baby's crib. These are powerful and majestic creatures whose radiance reflects the glory of the one they so adoringly worship and serve.

What's important, however, isn't who they are but *what* they do. They are mesmerized by the majesty of God, obsessed with his glory, and committed to unending and adoring praise. More on this below.

The lightning and thunder, undoubtedly quite literal, are also symbolic of God's awesome power and infinite might and remind us of the revelation of God at Mount Sinai (Exod. 19:16-18; 20:18-20). They may well be emanations of the endless energy of God's own being, pointing to the limitless depths of divine power. Some believe the seven spirits are a heavenly entourage of sorts that has a special ministry in the throne room. More likely, in view of the number 'seven' which often symbolizes divine perfection and completeness, this is the one Holy Spirit represented under the symbolism of a seven-fold or complete manifestation of his being.

The four living creatures remind us of the seraphim of Isaiah 6 and the cherubim of Ezekiel 1:5-25 and 10:1-22. Could they be symbolic of the created world itself, all of which is responsible to render praise to God? This is suggested by the number 'four' which points to the totality of the natural order: the four points of the compass, the four corners of the earth, and the four winds of heaven. Are they angels, or perhaps another 'species' of created, supernatural beings?

They are standing upon something that looks like a sea of glass resembling crystal (v. 6). Its surface stretches out before the throne to reflect the flashing light that proceeds from the character of God. They appear to stand in front, behind, and on either side of the throne (they are 'in the midst' of and 'around' the throne in 4:6, and 'before' the throne in 5:8; 19:4). Some suggest they are supporting the throne itself. Their focus is entirely on God, not each other or anything or anyone else in heaven.

The description of them in verse 7 may be designed to suggest qualities in the God they serve: the lion pointing to royal power; the calf/ox, a symbol of strength; the man, an expression of intelligence and spirituality; and the eagle, an embodiment of swiftness of action.

Their worship (v. 8) is *unending*: 'Day and night they never cease to say …' (cf. 14:11). As there is constant and perpetual punishment in hell, so there is constant and perpetual praise in heaven. The focus is on three of God's attributes. First, is his holiness, an echo of Isaiah 6. When Isaiah saw God for who he is, he saw himself as well. Knowledge of God always awakens a knowledge of oneself. God's holiness always exposes our sinfulness. But the holy God is also the gracious redeemer, for the hot coal applied to Isaiah's lips speaks of forgiveness and cleansing.

The God who captivates them is also sovereign. He is 'the Almighty' for he sits on the divine 'throne' (mentioned fourteeen times in this chapter, a symbol of divine authority and dominion and power). Well did the hymnwriter say:

God is still on the Throne,
and He will remember His own.
Though trials may press us
and burdens distress us,
He never will leave us alone.

God is still on the Throne,
He never forsaketh His own.
His promise is true,
He will not forget you,
God is still on the throne.

Mrs. F. W. Suffield

He is the eternal God 'who was and is and is to come' (cf. Exod. 3:14). Although timeless in his essential being, it must be noted that the phrase 'and is to come' points more to the impending return of God in the person of Jesus to consummate his kingdom than to the idea of eternal existence.

The praise that comes from the four living creatures gives way to that of the twenty-four elders (vv. 9-11). The word 'worship' means to fall prostrate at someone's feet. What gloriously appropriate repetition: *they fall down before him to fall down before him!* This is the first occurrence in Revelation of the paired verbs 'to fall down' and 'to worship' which are used to describe two stages of a single act of adoration and thus appear to be synonymous (they are also paired in 5:14; 7:11; 11:16; 19:10; 22:8; this combination is also found in Matt. 2:11; 4:9; 18:26; Acts 10:25; 1 Cor 14:25).

Why did the Elders fall face down? Over and over again, they hit the dirt, prostrate in God's presence (4:10; 5:8,14). Did one of the four living creatures shove them? Was it simply mechanical obedience to some heavenly liturgy? What did they see or hear or feel or believe or think that could have induced such an extravagant response? What possessed them to fall over and over and over again? No sooner do they stand than they fall! It isn't that they fall, come to their senses, and then stand, dusting themselves off, a little embarrassed for having momentarily lost their composure. No! They stand, then come to their senses, and fall! The only reasonable, rational, sensible thing to do is to fall down! They can't bear the thought of standing in the presence of such beauty and glory. Nothing would be more inappropriate or out of order than to remain upright and erect. They don't fall because they are wounded or weak or intimidated or fearful. They fall because they are stunned!

Why do the four living creatures not cease day or night from praising? Is it an expression of mere 'duty'? Is their adoration coerced or perhaps the fruit of bribery? Undoubtedly not! Consider every alternative. What else could possibly compare with the joy of unending adoration and delight in the splendor of God? No one put a gun to their head or threatened them with hell should they decline to worship. Why should they cease? For whom should they give up their praise? To do what? To go where? What can compare, what can rival, what can compete in its capacity to fascinate and fulfill and satisfy and entrance? Is there another more splendid? Is there another more beautiful?

True worship, such as we see in Revelation 4–5, is not simply unending, it is *uninhibited*. The atmosphere around the throne is charged with an unashamed exuberance. Physical expressions of delight and fear and joy and awe are commonplace. Unlike heaven, unfortunately, worship wars continue to rage in churches on every continent on earth. Whereas some enjoy the atmosphere of a Ringling Brothers Barnum & Bailey Circus, Sunday morning in other churches bears a striking resemblance to the county morgue! Your choice these days is often between the frenzy of unbridled chaos or the rigidity of immovable concrete.

Our personal preferences notwithstanding, *in heaven affections are ablaze for God. Bodies are prostrate in his presence. Praise is passionate. Enjoyment is extravagant. There is little, if any, fear of feelings.*

I'm surprised by how unsettling this is to some people. Could it possibly be due to their lack of familiarity with the central figures in Scripture? Consider, for example, David, King of Israel. Do you know why people love the psalms and seem always to return to them in time of need? Look no farther than the passion of their author, a man who virtually breathed holy desperation for God. A man whose heart beat with intense yearning and deep gratitude and a chronic longing for God's presence. A man who panted and thirsted and hungered for God and rejoiced and exulted and reveled in God. A man who was as exuberant in his celebration of righteousness as he was broken when injustice prevailed.

Or consider the apostle Paul. Although you may not think of him as an emotional or passionate person, there is hardly an epistle of his that does not drip with earnest longings of soul and spirit. His heart was ablaze with love for God and his mind flooded with high and exalted thoughts of his Savior. He happily spurned the comforts of this life, counting all things as refuse, esteeming them dung (Phil. 3:8) that he might experience the unparalleled thrill of knowing Jesus. He was constrained by love, often moved to tears of sympathy, and roused to holy anger by those who would bring harm to the church of Jesus Christ.

Paul's letters are filled with references to his overflowing affection for the people of God (2 Cor. 12:19; Phil. 4:1; 2 Tim. 1:2; and especially 1 Thess. 2:7-8). He speaks of his 'bowels of love' (Phil. 1:8 KJV; Philem. 12,20) for them, of his pity and mercy (Phil. 2:1), of his anguish of heart and the tears he shed for their welfare (2 Cor. 2:4), of his continual grief for the lost (Rom. 9:2), and of his enlarged heart (2 Cor. 6:11).

Surely Jesus himself was a passionate man greatly moved in heart and spirit with holy affection. He was not ashamed or hesitant to pray with 'loud cries and tears' (Heb. 5:7). The gospel writers speak of him as experiencing amazement, sorrow and grief (Mark 3:5), zeal (John 2:17), weeping (Luke 19:41-42), earnest desire (Luke 22:15), pity and compassion (Matt. 15:32; 18:33), anger (John 2:13-19), love (John 15:9), and joy (John 15:11). In Luke 10:21 he is said to have 'rejoiced in the Holy Spirit' as he was praying to the Father. He declared in John 15:11 and 17:13 that one of the principal aims in his earthly mission was to perfect the joy of his followers. Thus our joy is the joy of Jesus in us!

I don't believe it's possible to truly understand and appreciate the great things of God without being stirred with passion and zeal and joy and delight and fervor. Only obdurate spiritual blindness prevents the human soul from being greatly impressed and powerfully moved by the revelation of such eternal splendor.

The inhabitants of heaven feel compelled to cast down their crowns to acknowledge that any personal honor or power or authority is ultimately God's. They proclaim the Creator worthy of glory and honor and power because by his will 'they existed and were created' (literally, 'they were and they were created'; 4:11). But why the apparent illogical order of the verbs? How can the 'existence' of everything precede creation? In one sense, all things 'first' existed in God's mind and then came into being by God's will. Or perhaps the preservation of all things is mentioned before creation to encourage the persecuted people of God with the assurance that whatever befalls them is encompassed within their creator's ultimate purpose.

Redeemer!

Turn with me now to chapter five. I agree with G. B. Caird that 'the content of the *scroll* is God's redemptive plan, foreshadowed in the Old Testament, by which he means to assert his sovereignty over a sinful world and so to achieve the purpose of creation. John proposes to trace the whole operation of this plan from its beginnings in the Cross to its triumphal culmination in the new Jerusalem.'[2] The scroll contains the content, course, and consummation of history, how things will end for both Christian and non-Christian (see Ps. 139:16).

All creation in heaven and earth stands motionless and speechless as a search is undertaken for someone worthy to open this book. Is no one capable of bringing history to its ordained end? John's disappointment evokes a flood of tears as he contemplates the painful postponement of God's redemptive purposes. Is there no one who can take authority over history and insure that God's enemies will be judged and his people vindicated?

Thinking that he will see a lion, he is amazed to see a *lamb!* The fact that it is a 'lamb' points to his atoning sacrifice (Isa. 53:7; perhaps also the Passover Lamb is in view). Yet this lamb is 'standing, as though it had been slain', or more literally, 'slaughtered', with its throat cut. But if it is slain, how does it stand? Resurrection! This lamb bears both the marks of death and the marks of sovereignty, the 'seven horns' symbolizing perfect power as the Messianic conqueror and the 'seven eyes' referring to perfect wisdom.

Victory is achieved not by the sword but by a sacrifice. Jesus conquers through the cross! The power to change lives and orchestrate history flows from the love of a crucified carpenter.

The words 'in the midst of' (v. 6 KJV) could suggest that the Lamb is actually on the throne, surrounded by the four creatures and the twenty-four elders. But more likely the Lamb is standing near the throne, for in verse 7 he is portrayed as proceding to the throne and taking the book from the one who sits upon it. Again we see the consistent New Testament portrait of the Son at the right hand of his Father's throne.

In the presence of such redemptive splendor, there is only one appropriate response: singing! The 'prayers of the saints' (v. 8b) are more than simple requests or petitions for personal blessing. They are more than likely impassioned pleas for righteous retribution on the enemies of the church described later in 6:9-11 (and again in 8:4).

They sing a 'new' song (cf. Ps. 98:1-3; Isa. 42:10-13) because the Lamb has defeated the powers of evil and has inaugurated a new creation. And why is the lamb worthy of praise? Because he has died, and by dying has redeemed men and women from every corner of the earth, and by redeeming them has made them (i.e., you and me!) into a kingdom and into priests. We come to praise and worship God as *kings and priests in his kingdom*. I am here reminded, in awe yet again, of something my friend Mike Bickle has often said: 'What kind of God makes kings of his enemies?'

Suddenly there is a snowball effect that leads to an avalanche of praise. A holy turbulence engulfs the heavens. As the choir sings of God's majesty the adoration of the lamb moves out in ever-widening circles (see vv. 11-13). At first, it was the four living creatures singing their song of praise. They are then joined by the twenty-four elders. In verse 11 myriads and myriads and thousands and thousands of angels follow suit. And if that were not sufficient, we read in verse 13 that 'every creature in heaven and on the earth and under the earth and in the sea, and all that is in them' begin to praise the lamb! The seven-fold shout of worship in verse 12 rings out like the resounding chimes of a huge bell:

POWER! ... RICHES! ... WISDOM! ... MIGHT!
... HONOR! ... GLORY! ... BLESSING!

And even with that they do not cease ... verse 13!

When I read this inspired description of creaturely joy at the beholding of the Creator's glory, I am reminded of an anthropomorphic vision of God described by Jewish mystics of the fourth century. The ministering angels sing a paean to the face of God as they are stationed at their posts by the throne.

> *Lovely face, majestic face,*
> *face of beauty, face of flame,*
> *the face of the Lord God of Israel when he sits upon*
> *His throne of glory,*
> *robed in praise upon His seat of splendour,*
> *His beauty surpasses the beauty of the aged,*
> *His splendour outshines the splendour of newly-weds*
> *in their bridal chamber.*
>
> *Whoever looks at Him is instantly torn;*
> *whoever glimpses His beauty immediately melts away.*
> *Those who serve Him ... their hearts reel*
> *and their eyes grow dim at the splendour*
> *and radiance of their king's beauty.*[3]

And let us not forget, though some may prefer otherwise, that the God who is adored for his beauty and holiness and majesty in Revelation 4–5 is *the same God* who pours forth wrath and destruction and terror through the seal, trumpet, and bowl judgments. The same four living creatures who worship God in Revelation 4–5 also call forth the four horsemen of the first four seal judgments in 6:1ff. The seven trumpets are blown by the seven angels who stand before God in heaven (8:2,6).

And the designation of God in 4:9-10 as he 'who lives forever and ever' is found in 15:7 in connection with the 'bowls full of the wrath of God.' One can't escape the fact that the God whom the four living creatures happily and incessantly adore is the same God who manifests his righteous indignation and power in the terrifying judgments that bring history to its close.

Even more explicit is the literary link between the seventh of each series of judgments and the statement in 4:5a. In the latter we read of 'flashes of lightning, and rumblings and peals of thunder' issuing from the throne. This formula is then echoed at the opening of the seventh seal judgment (8:5), the sounding of the seventh trumpet (11:19), and the pouring out of the seventh bowl (16:18-21). In other words, the holiness of God described in Revelation 4–5 is most clearly manifested in the judgments on evil in the seals, trumpets, and bowls.

A Crucial Lesson

I earlier spoke of the relationship between celebration and elevation or between exultation and exaltation and argued that the former in each case is both a prelude to and grounds for the latter. There is, however, one additional stage in our experience that is antecedent to both exultation and exaltation, namely, *education*.

If we don't know who God is and how he thinks and what he feels and why he does what he does, we have no grounds for joy, no reason to celebrate, no basis for finding satisfaction in him. That is why our careful and meticulous study of the heavenly vision in Revelation 4–5 is so crucial to our lives as Christians.

Delight in God cannot occur in an intellectual vacuum. Our joy is the fruit of what we know and believe to be true of God. Emotional heat such as joy, delight, and gladness of heart, apart from intellectual light (i.e., the knowledge of God) is useless. Worse still, it is dangerous, for it inevitably leads to fanaticism and idolatry. The experience of heaven's inhabitants confirms that our knowledge of God (education) is the cause or grounds for our delight in him (exultation), which blossoms in the fruit of his praise and honor and glory (exaltation).

What this tells us is that *the ultimate goal of theology isn't knowledge, but worship*. If our learning and knowledge of God do not lead to the joyful praise of God, we have failed. *We learn only that we might laud*, which is to say that *theology without doxology is idolatry. The only theology worth studying is a theology that can be sung!*

A Glorious and Unending Reality!

What beauty! What transcendent glory! As for its depth, unfathomable. As for its duration, unending. As for its degree, immeasurable. As for its description, ineffable. This is a perpetual spiritual high from which you need never come down. Of it, and for us, there is only increase and expansion, eternal growth and endless intensity.

We must resist any inclination to disregard John's vision as irrelevant, as if it were but a distant dream, an ethereal far off heavenly phenomenon of which we on earth can only wonder. This is not *virtual* reality. This is no computer-generated facsimile. It is far more real than anything this temporal world can offer. The glory of the Holy Spirit is that he can take each syllable of this inspired portrait and set it ablaze that the fire of its truth and life-changing power might forever burn within our hearts. Thus may we be led to join the twenty-four elders and the four living creatures and the chorus of countless millions of angels, together with the redeemed even now in heaven, in the relishing and enjoyment of our great and glorious God!

[1] Warren Wiersbe, *Real Worship* (Nashville: Oliver Nelson, 1986), pp. 44-45.

[2] G. B. Caird, *A Commentary on the Revelation of St. John the Divine* (New York: Harper & Row, 1966), p. 72.

[3] Quoted in Patrick Sherry, *Spirit and Beauty: An Introduction to Theological Aesthetics,* 2nd edition (London: SCM Press, 2002), pp. 61-62.

Chapter Five
Galactic Grandeur

The heavens declare the glory of God,
and the sky above proclaims his handiwork.

Psalm 19:1

We are witnessing today a sad and strange phenomenon. It is epidemic in society at large and is making powerful inroads in the church as well. What is most frightening about this development is that many Christian leaders are either oblivious to it or know of it and applaud its growth. Many have even capitalized on its popularity and baptized it with religious language.

I'm talking about our obsessive preoccupation with the human soul. There is a sense in which the human soul has caved in on itself and is now held captive by a fixation with its own states and conditions and concerns. The soul has become parasitic on itself, feeding on its needs and cravings by excessive introspection and elaborate attempts to elevate its sense of self-worth.

Your soul was never meant for this. You were designed for something better. You were built for the contemplation of something infinitely more complex, something incomparably more fascinating than your own 'self'. You were created for the joyful contemplation of God.

Some think this is inconsistent with Christian Hedonism. How can I be an advocate for the 'soul's' pursuit of pleasure but an enemy of concern for 'self'? I can't! I'm not! What I oppose is the misguided and sinful assumption that what is best for my 'self' can be found in 'self'. I'm not denouncing concern for our 'souls' but only the misguided notion that 'self' is the solution to its own problem. Our concern for the state and happiness and destiny of our 'souls' is good, indeed, God-given. And it is given by God precisely because he invites us to feast our souls on his glory. The soul finds its greatest joy and most profound delight in the contemplation of God, not 'self'.

God created us out of the overflow of his goodness that we might share the incomparable joy he has in himself. There is nothing better or higher or more fulfilling for the human soul than this. Not in itself does the soul find satisfaction for itself. Not in its struggles, its fears, its feelings, or its triumphs but in God.

God has himself made it possible for us to do this. He spoke, and out of nothing leapt the universe! He thought, and galaxies appeared. He willed, and all that will ever be, was.

If you truly love your 'self' (and all of us do), take your eyes off 'self' and do your 'self' a favor: 'Look at me, says the Lord. The state and condition and circumstances of your soul will change for the good only to the degree that you make my glory the object of your obsession.' And where might this glory be seen? 'The *heavens*,' says David, 'declare the glory of God, and the sky above proclaims his handiwork' (Ps. 19:1).

Lift up your Eyes!

The implications of Psalm 19:1 and other texts like it have eluded us far too long. Here the psalmist alerts us to the sounds of a celestial symphony whose music never ends. This is a story whose plot complexities only increase and expand with the reading. This is a heavenly gallery of the most unimaginably exquisite and breathtaking art. The focus of it all is the majesty of God himself as he displays for our enjoyment and his glory the beauty of his creative artistry. Each of us is under a divine mandate to become an amateur astronomer, to peer into the incalculable depths of sky and space to behold the handiwork of our omnipotent Creator.

Simply saying God is infinite doesn't work. For us, infinity is at most whatever exceeds our atmosphere or transcends human ability. We rarely think of God as more than the creator of our globe and as dwelling somewhere beyond the solar system in a place called heaven. Our cognitive grid for understanding God's infinity does a horrible disservice to the term itself. The parameters of our thinking are so narrow and restricted that we risk reducing God to a dwarf whose glory is measured by human standards. No wonder God's capacity to win the affection of our hearts is in doubt.

What we need are measurements and models and a framework to which we can relate. To say that God is limitless in power and present throughout the universe is theologically true but experientially banal. I'm no scientist, but I want to invite you to come with me on a brief journey where most of you have never been before. Hold your breath and behold the beauty of your God!

How Fast is Fast?

I'm assuming most of you have traveled by air and can appreciate the speed with which we are now able to traverse not only our own country but the globe. Rarely will a commercial airplane fly at less than 500 miles per hour, so we will make that our consistent speed on the journey at hand.

That's actually quite slow, at least when compared with the speed of light. All of us learned in high school (or before) that light travels at an astonishing 186,000 miles per second (not per hour, but per *second!*). To be even more precise, it is 186,282.4 miles per second. We can convert that to 670,000,000 miles per hour! Not even my daughters drive that fast.

Don't let the magnitude of this escape you. It means that in one second a flash of light can travel around the entire earth seven times! Although our moon is 240,000 miles from earth, it takes light only one and one-third seconds to get from here to there. A brief moment to meditate on this simple but astounding feature of created reality will forever change how you read Genesis 1:3—"And God said, 'Let there be light,' and there was light." He could have created it even faster, but there is a point beyond which our brains can't compute.

An important measure that I'll mention on numerous occasions is the light-year. A light-year is how far light travels in one calendar year. If you've got a big calculator you can figure it out for yourself. Multiply 186,000 times 60 and you have a *light minute*. Multiply that figure by 60 and you have a *light hour*. Multiply that figure by 24 and you have a *light day*, and that by 365 and you have a *light year*. So, if light moves at 186,000 miles per second, it can travel six trillion miles (6,000,000,000,000) in a 365-day period. That's the equivalent of about 12,000,000 round trips to the moon. Now that's quick!

But let's return to our commercial 747 jet airline which pokes along at what now feels like a pathetically slow snail's pace of 500 mph. Buckle your safety belt and come with me on a journey you'll never forget.

How Far is Far?

Let's assume we are speeding in our jet airplane at 500 mph on a trip to the moon. If we traveled non-stop, twenty-four hours a day, it would take us just shy of three weeks to arrive at our destination. If we wanted to visit our sun, a mere 93 million miles from earth, it would take us a bit more than twenty-one years to get there. And if we wanted to reach Pluto, the planet farthest away in our solar system, our non-stop trip would last slightly longer than 900 years! Of course, we'd all be dead by then, but I trust you get the point.

If there is a clear sky tonight, go outside and gaze into the heavens. Pick a star, any star. It seems fairly close. Want to visit? Surely it couldn't take that long to get there. It almost seems you can extend your hand and touch it. Well, not quite. The nearest star to us is a system of three called Alpha Centauri. The closest of those is Proxima Centauri, a mere 4.3 light years from earth. If we were bored with Pluto and wanted to extend our journey, speeding along non-stop, twenty-four hours a day, seven days a week, fifty-two weeks a year, we would land on the closest star to earth in a mere six million years! That's 500 mph for 6,000,000 years. Beginning to get the picture?

Let's speed up our travel a bit. Suppose our airplane was fast enough to go from earth to the sun in only one hour. That's traveling at 93 million miles per hour. Imagine what that would do to the radar gun of your local police department! Traveling non-stop at 93 million mph, it would still take us over 78 years to reach 61 Cygni, a star in the constellation Cygnus (the Swan), roughly 10.9 light years from earth.

If you aren't satisfied with visiting a single star, perhaps you'd like to take a look at the next galaxy in our cosmic neighborhood. The Andromeda Galaxy is a giant spiral, almost a twin of our own Milky Way galaxy. Astronomers have determined that there's probably a black hole at its center one million times the mass of our sun.

Although Andromeda is closest to us it's still a staggering 2.5 million light years away (a mere 15 quintillion miles, or 15 with eighteen zeros). On dark nights in the fall it's barely visible to the naked eye as a small misty patch of light. Some are frightened to hear that it's moving toward us at 75 miles per second. No need to panic or rush to build a bomb shelter. At that pace, given its distance from earth, it might reach our Milky Way in about 6 billion years! Some say it will take only 3 billion years, so perhaps you should begin work on that bomb-shelter after all!

In case you're wondering (on the assumption that your brain is still able to calculate the seemingly incalculable), our trip to Andromeda would last a paltry 4.2 trillion years (that's 4,200,000,000,000 years).

This is the point where my mental circuits start shorting out. So let me wrap up this part of our journey with one more number. I recently purchased a poster bearing a photograph from the Hubble Space Telescope. It purports to show the most distant galaxy in the universe, at least the farthest one that Hubble has been able to detect. Astronomers estimate that it's approximately 13 billion light years from earth. Remember, a light year is 6,000,000,000,000 (six trillion) miles. That would put this galaxy at 78,000,000,000,000,000,000,000 miles from earth! In case you were wondering, we count from million, to billion, to trillion, to quadrillion, to quintillion, to sextillion. So, this galaxy is 78 sextillion miles from earth.

I can barely handle driving for more than three or four hours at 65 mph before I need to stop and do something, either eat at McDonald's or, well you know. The thought of traveling at 500 mph non-stop, literally sixty-minutes of every hour, twenty-four hours in every day, seven days in every week, fifty-two weeks in every year, with not a moment's pause or delay, for — are you prepared for this? — 20,000,000,000,000,000 years (that's 20 quadrillion years)! And that would only get us to the farthest point that our best telescopes have yet been able to detect. If the universe is infinite, as I believe it is, this would be the mere fringe of what lies beyond.

Here's one more for you to ponder. Shrink the earth to the size of a grapefruit. Pause for a moment and let the scale sink in. On this basis the moon would be a ping-pong ball about twelve feet away. The sun would be a sphere as big as a four-story building a mile away. Pluto would be an invisible marble thirty-seven miles away.

Now, put our entire solar system into that grapefruit. The nearest star would be over half a mile away. The Milky Way would span 12,000 miles! Now reduce the entire Milky Way to a grapefruit! The nearest galaxy to us, Andromeda, would be at a distance of ten feet. The Virgo cluster would be a football field away.

How Many is Many?

Now that we know how long it would take, what might we do to make the time pass more quickly? We can't count cars, as we might on a trip from Chicago to Dallas. Why don't we count stars? That ought to be easy enough. After all, most of us have tried to do that on a clear night from our backyard.

We must remember that our sun is but one star in but one solar system. Our solar system is part of a galaxy we call the Milky Way. The latter is approximately 100,000 light years in diameter. In other words, if you were somehow able to travel at the speed of light, 186,000 miles per second, it would take you 100,000 years to cross its span. It has a bulging core and flat, spiral arms. Just as planets circle the sun, the stars of the Milky Way orbit the galactic core, believed to enclose a gigantic black hole. Seen from far away the Milky Way looks like a giant pinwheel rotating slowly in space with four broad spiral arms bright with stars. Our sun, located about a quarter of the way out along one of these arms makes a complete circuit of the galaxy every 250 million years.

How many stars do you think are in our galaxy alone? The naked eye can see perhaps 4,000 stars on the best of nights. The Milky Way contains anywhere from 150 to 200 billion stars! And we are only one galaxy among some 150 billion others, each with tens upon tens of billions of stars. Each! There is a galaxy known as Virgo with more than 5 trillion stars all to itself.

Think of it this way. The next time you are at the beach, reach down and take into both hands as much sand as possible. Now begin to count! You'd probably lose track trying to count each granule and eventually go insane before half way through with your task. If you were to take every single, solitary grain of sand off of every square inch of beach on the face of the earth, you wouldn't equal the number of stars in the galaxies of the universe. And your God made them all! More amazing still, he named them all! The psalmist declared, 'He determines the number of the stars; he gives to all of them their names' (Ps. 147:4). No wonder the very next verse proclaims, 'Great is our Lord, and abundant in power; his understanding is beyond measure' (Ps. 147:5). What an understatement!

How Big is Big?

Our sun, a mere 864,000 miles in diameter, is actually a bit puny, as stars go. Comparatively tiny though it be, you could line up more than 100 earths, each touching the next, and still not span the diameter of the sun. You can make 333,000 earth sized planets from the matter in the sun. Whereas the surface temperature is 5,500° C, its central temperature is 15,000,000 degrees Celsius. Ouch!

Astronomers have been especially focused on one of the biggest stars in our galaxy known as Eta Carinae (pronounced either 'ate-a car-EYE-nee' or 'etta CAR-a-nie'). This star lies in the far southern sky and can't be seen from much of the northern hemisphere. The diameter of Eta Carinae is a bit more than 400 million miles. If it stood in for our sun it would swallow up all the planets out to Mars! It's only 7,500 light years away in a spiral arm of the Milky Way.

As the heaviest star in our galaxy, Eta Carinae is in serious need of a diet, tilting the scales at a svelte 120 times the mass of the sun. In 1848 it ejected a huge dumbbell-shaped cloud of gas and dust that is visible to this day. We're not talking about your typical cloud that might cast its shadow over a city. This nebula is about twice the width of our entire solar system!

Twinkle, twinkle *little* star, it ain't! In addition to its size and weight, Eta Carinae is so bright that if it were 185 billion miles away (more than fifty times the distance to Pluto) it would still shine as brightly as our sun does being only 93 million miles away!

If that isn't big enough for you, I recently read that astronomers found a mysterious object at least forty billion times as massive as the sun. Some say it's closer to 200 billion times! This is either the largest black hole ever or some new unexplained phenomenon. The mass of this object is equal to that of all the stars in the Milky Way galaxy combined (that's 150 billion stars), yet it is compressed into a space 10,000 times smaller.

How Bright is Bright?

If we learn anything from Eta Carinae it is that one should never travel in space without some heavy-duty shades and high quality sun block!

Astronomers recently discovered what they've called the Pistol Star, which glows with the energy of 10 million of our suns. That's right. Not 10, not 100, not even 1,000, but 10,000,000 suns. Believe it or not, that's actually pretty dim when compared with some other objects in our universe.

The brightest star burst ever was recently discovered. Trying to explain the amount of energy released by this explosion is itself no small task, but here goes. The energy emitted would correspond to 10,000 times the energy produced by our sun— over its entire lifetime! Some believe our sun is 5 billion years old. So, add up all the energy emitted by the sun over the last 5 billion years, now multiply it by 10,000, and that's how much energy was emitted by this recent blast!

Quasars are the highly energetic cores of extremely distant spiral galaxies. The first quasars were discovered in the 1960s. They must be the loneliest objects in the sky because they are so powerful that if you came within 1,200,000,000,000,000 miles of one you would be vaporized. That's 1.2 quadrillion miles! Some quasars radiate as much energy as a thousand of our Milky Ways, yet take up little more space than our solar system.

There is a quasar labeled 3C-273 that is approximately 2,700 million light years from earth. This one quasar radiates more than 100 times as much visible power as all the stars in the Milky Way combined! That's 100 times the brightness of 150 billions stars! Sound impressive? Another quasar, 3C-48, is 3.7 billion light years from earth and radiates a light 1,000 times that of the entire Milky Way from a volume less than one-hundred-thousandth of its size.

There is a constellation named Cassiopeia that is 10,000 light years away or a mere 60 quadrillion miles (that's 60 with 15 zeros). In this constellation there was a star named Cassiopeia A. I say 'was' because it blew up about 320 years ago. Isaac Newton is thought to have actually seen the light from this supernova. Do you know how bright Cassiopeia A was when it exploded? I'll be honest. I don't like summer. Every day we read a new report of the dangers of extended exposure to our sun's rays. I much prefer the cool of November, even the sub-freezing temperatures of January. I've been known to complain about the heat in August. When the thermometer hits 90 I feel scorched, notwithstanding the fact that the sun is 93 million miles away. So get hold of this. When Cassiopeia A exploded it shined with a brightness of 100 billion of our suns! Talk about tanning.

How Powerful is Powerful?

The Crab Nebula was once a massive star about 6,000 light years from earth in the constellation Taurus. The star blew up over a thousand years ago forming the nebula. The light from the explosion was first seen by astronomers in China in 1054. Moments before the explosion the star's core was compressed into an extremely dense and rapidly spinning ball of atomic particles known as neutrons. That ball remained after the blast and is only twelve miles across but is quite dense. If you've ever been frustrated, as I have, with electrical power failures and light bulbs that don't last, you'll appreciate this. It puts out a constant 10 quadrillion volts of electricity. Is that a lot, you ask? Let's put it this way. Envision your typical lightning bolt—and multiply it 30 million times!

I also read of another supernova's collapse and the energy it released. Although I was born six years after the end of World

War II I've seen considerable film footage of atomic bombs like those dropped on Nagasaki and Hiroshima. The magnitude of those explosions and the horrifying mushroom clouds are indelibly printed on our national conscience. Now imagine an explosion that released the energy of 10,000,000 Hiroshima bombs! Don't stop now. There's more. Imagine that 10,000,000 Hiroshima bombs explode simultaneously on each of 100,000,000 stars in our galaxy! That's how much energy was produced by this one supernova! I have to ask: What are your thoughts of a God who could pull this off without the slightest effort or loss of energy? Is that kind of God able to meet your needs and satisfy your soul and supply you with all good things? It sounds like a silly question now, but it needed to be asked.

Astronomy magazine's issue of November, 2001 (p. 24) described a planetary nebula known as the Red Spider Nebula that is some 3,000 light years away in Sagittarius. It contains the indescribably hot core of a dead sun-like star. I say it is indescribable because it is 900,000 degrees Fahrenheit. This stellar remnant is so hot that winds traveling at 9,000,000 miles per hour (talk about the makings of a 'bad hair' day!) erupt from its surface and slam into the surrounding nebular material to create enormous waves more than 62 billion miles high. These waves, traveling at more than 500,000 mph make the fifty-foot waves on Hawaii's shores look pathetic. Try surfing that one!

Black holes are a fascinating and bewildering subject, having made their way into our most recent Hollywood sci-fi adventures. But there is nothing fictional about these cosmic cannibals that eat anything that dares venture near. A black hole is the final stage of life of very massive stars. Eventually the inward pull of gravity increases to such a degree that the star collapses in on itself.

Black holes are so small (about the size of a pea) and dense that nothing, not even light, can escape from the immense gravitational pull at their surfaces. And remember, light is fast—traveling at 186,000 miles per second. Yet, if you were to stand at its event horizon (the spherical 'boundary', so to speak, of a black hole) and flash a beam of light away from a black hole, the light would turn and be consumed by the hole.

How Heavy is Heavy?

Every four years we watch with amazement as Olympic weightlifters jerk, snatch, and squat an incredible number of pounds. We cringe as all too often one of them buckles beneath the bar, perhaps snapping a bone or tearing a muscle. Lifting a car or a house is something we leave to massive machinery. Lifting the entire earth is beyond our capacity to see or think.

So I ask, how heavy are the heavens? I've noted the remarkable size of stars and the like, but what do they weigh? Stars come in all sizes, some of which are 50 million times the mass of earth![1] And there are 150 billion galaxies, each of which contains tens if not hundreds of billions of stars! What's holding it all up? Better still, Who's holding it up? God is, of course! Yet he never breaks a sweat. He never groans under the strain. His knees never buckle or his muscles cramp. He holds not one, nor several, but all of the billions and billions and billions of stars in the sky. He does it effortlessly. He merely thinks and they all stand firm. Such is the nature of divine power and strength and might.

There are what are called white dwarf stars whose density belies their name. They contain matter one million times as dense and hard as steel! One in particular is named Sirius B. It has a density one million times that of Earth, which is to say, 1,000 tons per cubic inch, equal to 2,000,000 pounds.

Of all the sizes and shapes and weights in the universe, I'm fascinated by neutron stars. They are actually quite small, as stars go, often no more than ten miles across. Yet such tiny stars contain more mass than our sun! This may stretch you beyond belief, but one *teaspoonful* of this matter weighs 3 billion tons. That's not a misprint. That's 6 trillion pounds (6 with 12 zeroes). How does one compute 6 trillion pounds? How does one put it in words or images that make sense to us? Here's one way. It's the equivalent of stuffing a herd of 50 million elephants in a thimble! If we dropped a small piece of a neutron star onto the ground it would slice through the earth like a bullet through cotton and come out the other side. Who made it? Who holds it in place? Yahweh, our God, 'brings out their host by number', calls 'them all by name' and insures that 'not one [of them] is missing' (Isa. 40:26).

One final illustration of the incredible size and weight of celestial objects is the comet. The Hale-Bopp comet came within eyesight in the spring of 1997. I stood on my balcony in Grandview, Missouri and watched it pass. Although it may have looked small to us on earth, it contained enough water to fill all the Great Lakes!

In the spring of 1996 the Comet Hyakutake stretched across the sky, amazing all by the length of its tail. At such a great distance away it is often hard to grasp how long a comet's tail might be. This one was a mere 350 million miles.

How Much Can God Lift?

After talking about such massive weight, I can't help but think of the age-old conundrum: *can God create a stone too heavy for God to lift?* Ronald Nash articulates the problem this way:

> *If God can create the stone too heavy for God to lift, there is something God cannot do (namely, lift the stone). And if God cannot create the stone too heavy for him to*

lift, there is still something he cannot do (in this case, cre-
ate the stone). Either God can or cannot create such a stone.
Therefore, in either case, there is something God cannot
do; and in either case, we seem forced to conclude that God
is not omnipotent.[2]

But for this objection to hold, it must propose a 'thing', a
genuine 'task' for God to do. And it doesn't. The request that
'*the Being who can do anything, which includes creating and*
lifting all stones, create a stone too heavy to be lifted by the
Being who can lift any created thing' is incoherent. It proposes
nothing. It's a pseudo-task. That is to say, *a stone too heavy to*
be lifted by him who can lift all stones is contradictory. Likewise,
for God to create something which is a nothing (namely, a stone
too heavy to be lifted by him who can lift all stones), is
contradictory. That God cannot create a stone which logically
cannot be created is no more a threat to omnipotence than his
alleged 'inability' to create a round triangle. Thus, praise be to
God who can do all things!

Behold, your God!

Pause with me for a moment and reflect on what's been said.
No words have been found that can adequately express the
magnitude of this universe we call home. Yet the vast, immense,
incalculable, unfathomable size of what I've just described would
be, at best, a microscopic speck on the tip of God's outstretched
finger! Oh, the majesty, the splendor, the immeasurable glory
of a God so great that he made it, sustains it, and points to it as
the revelation of his ineffable beauty.

Resist the temptation to think such scientific facts are ethereal
bits of irrelevant data that have no bearing on who you are and
how you live. God himself encourages us to look on them and

ponder their magnitude, especially in those seasons of life when he seems distant, remote, uninvolved, and worst of all, apathetic.

When God asks a question, we'd do well to provide an answer. This is precisely what happens in Isaiah 40. "To whom then will you compare me, that I should be like him?" says the Holy One (Isa. 40:25). This rhetorical question became necessary as some in Israel were being seduced by other gods. They yielded under pressure to compare Yahweh with the deities of Babylon, having been told that another was equal to or even better than he, more able and willing to help, and above all, more caring.

God is up to the challenge. 'Lift up your eyes on high and see: who created these?' (Isa. 40:26). If only for a moment, take your eyes off yourself and your circumstances, off the ways of this world and all rival claimants, and look at who God is. Ponder his mighty deeds. This isn't to say your soul or circumstances aren't important. It simply means that you are in the hands of an omnipotent God whose ability to act on your behalf is equaled only by his passionate affection for you as his child, whose strength is without end and whose sovereignty covers the expanse of the heavens. God's desire isn't to minimize your life and struggles and disappointments. His intent is for you to gain hope, knowing that nothing can wrench you from the loving arms of a God like this!

The Canaanites believed that heavenly bodies were visible representations of deities or gods (see 2 Kings 17:16; 21:3; Amos 5:26; Jer. 7:18; 8:2; 44:17). This is why Moses issued the command in Deuteronomy 4:19 that we not bow down and serve the sun, moon, and stars. Far from being worthy of worship, they aren't even self-existent. They are created and sustained by God, subservient to his will.

In Isaiah 40:26, four things are said. First, God created them. When once there was nothing, save God, he spoke and they leapt into being. The only reason why there's something rather than nothing is because God said so. Second, he 'brings out their host by number'. They stand at attention, as it were, and are set in place according to his sovereign decree. Third, he calls them all by name, reflecting his creative right of ownership. Finally, because of 'the greatness of his might, and because he is strong in power, not one is missing'.

So why do you continue to complain that your 'way is hidden from the Lord' and that he has disregarded the justice due to you (v. 27)? Isaiah puts in our mouths the question we all ask: 'Where is God? Why doesn't he care? Why doesn't he do something about this mess I'm in? Can't he see this injustice I'm enduring? Why doesn't he take action? Why won't he intervene? Doesn't he love me anymore? Does he even know my name? Does he know where I live and what I do every day? Or is he just incompetent?'

Isaiah is incredulous at such murmuring. 'Have you not known? Have you not heard? The LORD is the everlasting God, the Creator of the ends of the earth. He does not faint or grow weary; his understanding is unsearchable' (v. 28). Just creating the stars would be exhausting. Naming every single one of the trillions and trillions and trillions of them would be indescribably wearisome. Then think about trying to *remember* them all! Does God have a supernatural rolodex? Do they wear nametags? And then on top of all that, he exerts sufficient power and strength to hold them all in place!

Yet, God never gets tired! His energy never diminishes! God is as infinitely energetic after doing all that as he was before he started. He's never tuckered out. He never says, 'Boy, I'm wasted.' God never gets pooped!

How can this be? It's because God is the uncreated creator. He's everlasting, without beginning or end. You and I may know him, but we will never exhaustively figure him out. His mind and his ways are inscrutable. This is no abstraction. This is no ethereal perspective on life. This is your God!

The good news is that God isn't greedy with His strength. He's generous and will share with us all whatever we need. 'He gives power to the faint, and to him who has no might he increases strength' (Isa. 40:29). Amazing! After all he's done he retains an infinite supply of power to give to others. You never hear God say to someone who draws near: 'I'm so sorry. I'd like to help. But I've used up all my energy with these darn stars. If I hadn't made so many of them perhaps I wouldn't be in this predicament. This was a slight miscalculation on my part. I won't let it happen again. Maybe you should come back in a week or so after I've had time to catch up on my sleep and get my batteries recharged.' No!

In verse 30 Isaiah takes as an example the most energetic and strong and durable individual on earth: the young man, most likely the athlete or soldier who isn't hampered by the onset of old age. Humans at their peak and pinnacle still have limited resources. If the best we have to offer eventually wears down, what hope is there in anything humans can do or provide?

But we mustn't despair, for 'they who wait for the LORD shall renew their strength; they shall mount up with wings like eagles; they shall run and not be weary; they shall walk and not faint' (Isa. 40:31).

This isn't passive inactivity, but diligent, desperate, perseverance. Waiting on God entails three elements: (1) complete dependence on him (embracing the truth of what he has just said and actively entrusting one's soul and circumstances to the God who does what he says he does); (2) yielding to his schedule, i.e., patiently acquiescing to the wisdom of his timing, not ours; and (3) seeking God's face, pressing in to know him better and to love him more.

This is an unnatural strength that comes to otherwise helpless people. A supernatural strength that makes ordinary, weak people seem as if they can go on and on and on as effortlessly as the eagle soars above. And it all began by looking up, by beholding the beauty of God in the heavens he has made.

Wherever I turn I hear the all too familiar complaint: 'I need more faith. If only I could believe.' Tragically, the best counsel they get is to look inward, to search their souls, to castigate their spirit, to wrench their wills, with the hope that a mere drop of faith might ooze out and get them over the hump.

But consider what we've learned in this chapter. Do you realize how easily faith comes when you have a God like this? We struggle to believe that God is up to the task of handling our lives. Can he really be trusted? Does he have it in him to pull it off? Is he sufficiently glorious to warrant my worship? Is he really worth forsaking all else?

When you find yourself falling into doubt, simply lift up your eyes on high and gaze upon his handiwork. Listen to the heavens sing. Bend an ear to the story of the stars. Behold your God!

---

[1] Just in case you were wondering, the earth weighs in at just under 13,000,000,000,000,000,000,000,000 pounds!

[2] Ronald H. Nash, *The Concept of God* (Grand Rapids: Zondervan, 1983), p. 47.

Chapter Six
Microscopic Majesty

For by him all things were created, in heaven and on earth,
visible and invisible, ... and in him all things hold together.

Colossians 1:16-17

I admit it sounds pretty weird at first, but there's something stunning about prepositions. That's right, *prepositions*. I'm really not nuts. Trust me. Yes, I'm talking about those words like 'in' and 'over' and 'through' and 'by' and 'for', just to mention a few. There is immeasurable spiritual wealth in those little words. I'm fascinated to think that God would entrust the revelation of his glory to something as mundane as prepositions, words that few of us ever pause in the course of a day to notice. But the more I meditate on prepositions the more I see the beauty and majesty of Jesus. Let me prove it to you.

When Christians gathered for worship in the early church they sang hymns of praise like we do. Most scholars agree that the words to one such hymn are used by Paul in Colossians 1:15-17. Read it closely and take special note of the italicized prepositions it contains:

He is the image of the invisible God, the firstborn of all creation. For by [literally, in] him all things were created, in heaven and on earth, visible and invisible, whether thrones or dominions or rulers or authorities—all things were created through him and for him. And he is before all things, and in him all things hold together.

Perhaps an analogy will help make my point. Consider the stages involved in building a home. The first thing you do is hire an architect who draws up the blueprints. He formulates the plan and lists the many specifications on how everything is to be constructed. You then contract a builder, the person who actually puts brick to mortar and nail to wood. The house is then put to the use for which it was built: you move in. You occupy it and enjoy the many special features it contains, whether a special den or a hot-tub on the deck. Finally, as its inhabitant and owner, you maintain it. You are careful to make timely repairs and perhaps a bit of remodeling here and there.

Here's my point. Jesus Christ is all of these in relation to the whole of the universe! He is the architect. This is what Paul means in Colossians 1:16a when he says that all things were created 'in' him. He is the artisan. He is the one in whose eternal mind the blueprints for every nook and cranny of the cosmos were conceived. And Paul is pretty specific about the extent of Christ's creative input. It encompasses literally everything: 'all things' (v. 16a), by which he means everything 'in heaven and on earth', be they massive galaxies billions of light years away or the dust mites beneath your feet. The 'all things' includes what you can see and can't see, whether visible but intangible, like a mirage or beam of light; whether invisible but tangible, like a summer breeze or the heat of the sun; whether visible and tangible, like an oak tree or the book you now hold in your hand; even things invisible and intangible like a proton or gravity or a feeling or a dream. He conceived them all!

But it doesn't stop there. He is the architect of every spiritual being, here described as 'thrones' and 'dominions' and 'rulers' and 'authorities,' typical Pauline language for every conceivable variety of angel, both good and evil, both hellish and holy. They were all Christ's idea!

He is not only the architect who conceived their existence and their manifold properties and powers, he is the artisan who actually constructed their being. They were made *through* him, says Paul (v. 16b). John echoed this thought by saying that 'all things were made through him, and without him was not any thing made that was made' (John 1:3).

Yes, he is both architect and artisan, as well as the *aim* for which they were created. As Paul put it, 'all things were created ... *for* him' (Col. 1:16c; oh blessed preposition!). Whatever is, is, that he might be glorified and praised and enjoyed forever. He's the reason, the goal, the aim, the intent, the point, the purpose, the end, the terminus, the consummation and culmination of every molecule that moves.

If that weren't enough, he's also the sustaining and supportive power by which all that he has conceived and constructed should stay in being. He didn't create, only to skip town. From the moment of its inception until now and for so long as he so wills Jesus sustains all things, guides all things, and is in process of providentially bringing all things to their proper consummation in and for him. This is Paul's point in Colossians 1:17 when he says that the Son of God who was 'before' all things is the one 'in' whom all things 'hold together'.

Jesus is the cohesive power that keeps all things intact. If I may say it reverently, he's the 'divine glue' that holds it all in place. This world is a cosmos rather than a chaos because of the continuous exertion of divine power from the risen Christ! The things that are don't exist by virtue of some power intrinsic to themselves. Cars and chairs and baseballs and butter and quarks and quasars and, yes, everything, exist and are sustained in their present form by virtue of the incessant energy emanating from Jesus! If at any moment, for any reason, he should loosen his providential and preserving grip on any thing, it would disintegrate. It would vaporize and vanish into a vacuum of nothingness.

Every heartbeat, every flutter of an eyelid, every rustle of every blade of grass, every breath you breathe is sustained by the Son of God. Truly did Paul say in Acts 17:28 that 'in Him we live and move and have our being'.

We can wake up each day confident that we will not freeze to death because in the sun, that we so easily take for granted, hundreds of billion billion billion billion (that's 10 with 38 zeros) fusion reactions take place every second. More than 400,000,000 tons of hydrogen are being converted into helium every second in the heart of the sun. And this is only one sun among billions of trillions of others, all of which are a constant inferno of chemical and nuclear reactions, all of which are the product of the power and sustaining energy of Jesus who sits enthroned at the right hand of God.

Seeing the Creator in the Creation

This means that the physical world is a window to the beauty of God. Nature or creation or the cosmos, however you wish to put it, is here, not primarily that we might exploit its resources to enhance our comfort, nor as a means to expand our control over those weaker than ourselves, nor as merely the platform on which we might live out our desires and fulfill our personal vision. The physical world exists pre-eminently to display for our eternal joy the artistic creativity, endless power, and manifold wisdom of its Creator, the Son, our Lord Jesus Christ.

The apostle Paul said as much in his letter to the Romans. God's 'invisible attributes', wrote Paul, 'namely, his eternal power and divine nature, have been clearly perceived, ever since the creation of the world, in the things that have been made' (Rom. 1:20). The intended effect of this divinely-initiated self-revelation of eternal glory (Rom. 1:23) was that we might revel in the joy of honoring God (Rom. 1:21) and celebrate him with reverent gratitude for the mercy he displayed in making known such beauty to hell-deserving creatures (Rom. 1:21). But alas, sin intervened (read Paul's description of its impact in Romans 1:21-32).

Sin's presence, though, has not diminished the display of divine glory. Countless texts in both testaments bear witness to the multitude of ways in which the splendor of God is seen in nature (see Psalms 8:1-4; 19:1-6; 29; 104; 147; and 148 for just a few examples). In the previous chapter we saw this in the vast dimensions of space and speed and stars and supernova.

But our God is Creator and Lord not simply over the heavens and the planets and the quasars and the spiral galaxies that lie billions of light years away. He is also Creator and Lord and God over the infinitesimally tiny universe of sub-atomic particles. He is Creator and Lord over the biggest and the smallest, over the most massive and the most minute, from the gargantuan to the ineffably diminutive elements of all that is.

It's a Small World After All

I've always enjoyed those decorative Russian *matrioshka* dolls that fit one inside the other, each revealing yet one more, still smaller, version of whatever preceded it. There's a sense in which the same is true of nature. Each time we peel back yet another layer of matter there is yet another, even smaller, level of reality. If your heart was overwhelmed by the grandeur of the galaxies and the God who made them, consider now the sub-atomic world of particle physics. It's a stunner!

The story begins in ancient Greece. One of the first to make an effort at explaining the fundamental building block of nature was the philosopher Thales who died in 547 B.C. He believed the basic substance of all things was water. Anaximenes, insisted it was air. A hundred years passed before Democritus (460-370 B.C.) and Leucippus (480-420 B.C.) argued that all matter is composed of indivisible particles that they inappropriately named 'atoms'. I say 'inappropriately' because the word atom is derived from the Greek for 'that which cannot be divided or cut'.

For centuries following these early Greek thinkers it was believed that the atom was the smallest particle in nature. We now know that each atom has its own nucleus in which are found even smaller electrically charged particles known as protons and neutrons, around which constantly swirls an orbit of what are called electrons (there are as many electrons as protons in every atom).

Inside the Atom

All atoms are roughly the same size, namely, very, very, very tiny. How tiny? Well, try to wrap your mind around this. Let's take a simple and relatively small length of measure that everyone can envision, such as one inch. That's about the length of the sub-heading above in which are found a mere thirteen letters.

The question I want to pose is this: How many atoms can you line up in a row, side by side, in the space of an inch? More than thirteen, I assure you. I've heard countless answers, ranging from a thousand to ten thousand to a million. That we should think in such pathetically paltry amounts reflects how little we know of the creative power of God.

Would you believe that in the span of one inch you can line up, side by side, approximately 100,000,000 atoms? That's one-hundred million! In other words, it would take 10,000,000,000,000,000,000,000,000,000 atoms to make a typical cat. Why anyone would want to make a typical cat escapes me, but there you have it (I'm a dog lover).

Perhaps the most startling thing about the typical atom isn't its incredibly small size but the fact that it consists largely of empty space. What little mass there is of an atom is found in its *nucleus*. The nucleus of each atom is considerably smaller. 'Considerably' is a poor choice of words, but I'm running out of adjectives! When things get this tiny the best we can do is appeal to an illustration. So try this.

Think of an atom as if it were a typical football stadium, like the Rose Bowl in Pasadena, California. If such were an atom, the nucleus would be the size of a single grain of sand on the fifty-yard line. If it helps to put a number on it, here goes. The nucleus of an atom comprises only one part in 100,000,000,000,000, that's one part in 100 trillion! Now that's tiny!

The implications of this are stunning. It means, for example, that the chair in which you're sitting and the ground on which the chair rests and the cup of coffee on your right and the lamp on the left are all predominantly empty space, a vacuum, if you will. The multitude of atoms that comprise any particular piece of matter are like the balloon you blew up at your kid's birthday party. But only 'like' the balloon because there is something inside. That brings us back to the nucleus.

The typical atom is a giant of unimaginable proportions in comparison with that particle which constitutes its mass. Let's go back to our inch and see how many nuclei (that's plural for nucleus) we can line up in a row, side by side. We were able to line up 100,000,000 atoms inside the parameters of our inch. That's a mere pittance compared to the number of nuclei that would fit. Try this on for size (pardon the pun). Would you believe 10,000,000,000,000,000,000,000? That's 10 with 21 zeros, or, 10 sextillion!

Let's pause, catch our breath, and reflect on what I've said. In this universe that your God, the eternal lover of your soul, has made, there are particles so small that it would take 10 sextillion of them to fill an inch of space!

Quirky Quarks

Believe it or not, it gets better. Or, to be more accurate, it gets smaller! As I said, the atom is like one of those Russian dolls. Just when you thought you'd found the last one, you open it up and find yet another. In the case of a typical atom we've already noted the existence of its nucleus. But in the nucleus there's yet more, for each contains particles called protons and neutrons, sometimes as many as 200, with a bevy of electrons swirling around them. Protons carry a positive electrical charge and neutrons do not (hence their name). Comparatively speaking, the mass of the neutron is greater than that of a proton by a mere 0.14 percent, but both are about 2,000 times heavier than an electron.

I won't bother trying to explain how many protons you can line up inside an inch.[1] I'll just move on to what's inside them. We are now approaching the end of the line, so to speak. The last of the Russian dolls is near. Physicists believe that inside each proton and neutron are three infinitesimally small particles called *quarks*. It's a funny name coined by physicist Murray Gell-Mann (b. 1929). Actually, he didn't coin it, but he was a fan of James Joyce (1882-1941) who used the phrase 'three quarks for Muster Mark' in his book *Finnegans Wake*. Now you know.

A proton has two 'up' quarks and one 'down' quark (the names 'up' and 'down' don't signify anything important), whereas it's the other way around for neutrons. And quarks, we are told, are less than one-thousandth the size of the proton or neutron in which they're found. Physicists now believe that quarks are the fundamental building blocks of all matter. Quite simply, it doesn't get any smaller than a quark. That could change, of course. There's always room for a new discovery. But for now we'll stop our journey with the quark.

Your average nucleus in your average atom might contain as many as 1,000 quarks. Now remember, a quark is less than one-thousandth the size of the proton or neutron in which it's found. So, here we go one more time: Do you know how many quarks you can line up in a row, side by side, inside the space of one inch? Would you believe 10,000,000,000,000,-000,000,000,000? That's 10 with 24 zeros, or 10 septillion!

The sub-atomic particle world is yet more crowded (although at their size I hardly think they'd complain of a lack of space!). Physicists do have a sense of humor. They appropriately call a *gluon* the force that binds quarks together! Then there are *muons* which I won't even begin to line up in our inch because they don't stay around long enough to let us count them. Muons are identical to electrons but 200 times heavier. As I said, they don't hang around very long. In fact, muons aren't born with much of a future. Within 2 millionths of a second after a muon is produced, it explodes into electrons and neutrinos. Think about it: if every muon in the universe dies within 2 millionths of a second after its birth, the energy output necessary to keep up their production must be beyond our wildest dreams or capacity to calculate. Big God!

But what are *neutrinos*? The Italian physicist Enrico Fermi (1901-1954) first named this particle a neutrino, which means 'small neutron' in Italian. Neutrinos are electrically neutral particles, the size of which is simply mind-boggling. I find it odd that we would even use the word 'size' when talking about them. They are only one millionth the mass of the electron and the electron has a mass only $1/1836$ that of the proton. A supernova that was detected in 1987 produced an amazing number of neutrinos upon exploding. I would take up too much space to write the number so I'll describe it: 10 to the 58th power! That is, 10 with 58 zeroes behind it!

Growing up, I had two heroes: Mickey Mantle and Superman. The former had numerous limitations, the latter only one. He couldn't see through lead, apparently due to its incredible density. Neutrinos would laugh at our visitor from the planet Krypton, given the fact that they can pass through trillions of miles of lead without so much as a twitch of deviation from their appointed path. You and I aren't made of lead, but in the time it has taken me to define what a neutrino is, some 60 trillion of those little suckers ejected into space by the sun will have passed through your body without touching a thing, without leaving a trace of their travel, without you feeling the slightest tickle!

Feeling High-Strung

As I said, most physicists now believe that quarks are the fundamental building blocks of all matter. Although quarks are far too small to be seen even by the most sophisticated technology, there's good reason to believe they are there.

The most recent theory to come forth concerning the nature of a quark is that it's not a dimensionless circular point in space. In other words, the quark isn't like the dot of the letter 'i'. Rather, somewhat like an infinitely thin rubber band, or extremely fine strand of spaghetti, a quark is an incredibly tiny one-dimensional loop or string that vibrates or oscillates in a peculiar way depending on the kind of particle. Your basic string loop would be around a hundred billion billion (that's 10 with 19 zeroes) times smaller than your typical atomic nucleus.

If this theory is correct, and physicists aren't entirely sure, everything in the universe, from the gargantuan quasars in the heavens to the lady bug that appears in the spring to the food you'll eat for lunch today, is simply the visible product of a seemingly infinite number of infinitesimally tiny, vibrating filaments! Brian Greene, whose best-selling and intriguing book *The Elegant Universe* I mentioned in Chapter One, put it best in saying that 'if string theory is right, the microscopic fabric of our universe is a richly intertwined multidimensional labyrinth within which the strings of the universe endlessly twist and vibrate, rhythmically beating out the laws of the cosmos.'[2] What Greene fails to note is that there is a maestro of majestic power who not only leads this magnificent symphony of strings but created each one and fine-tunes their music to the glory of his own name.

Still More Holes

We looked briefly at the subject of black holes in the previous chapter. But have you ever thought of becoming one? It's theoretically possible for any object to become a black hole if it is compressed sufficiently. Trinh Xuan Thuan explains that 'if you weigh 160 pounds, and if a giant hand were to shrink your size to ... 10 billion times smaller than an atomic nucleus, you would become a black hole. In fact, the size down to which an object has to be compressed is proportional to its mass. If you want to turn a 1,600 pound elephant – that is, ten times more than your own mass – into a black hole, you will have to squash it down to ... ten times larger than in the case of your own distinguished person.'[3]

American physicist John Wheeler (b. 1911), who introduced the term 'black hole' to physics, also dubbed another strange phenomenon a 'wormhole'. These are like black holes but they have no event horizons which when crossed preclude the possibility of turning back. Assuming they exist, and no one knows for sure, they would function like a 'bridge or tunnel that provides a shortcut from one region of the universe to another'.[4] Thuan points out that what makes wormholes so fascinating is that they make it theoretically possible to travel through time. 'Enter a wormhole one way, and you will go into the future. Proceed in the opposite direction, and you will return to the past.'[5] But don't get too excited. There are numerous problems to overcome before we can become Trekkies or experience what Michael J. Fox did in *Back to the Future*.

Perhaps the biggest obstacles are the size of wormholes and their remarkably short life span. Wormholes are 10 with 33 zeros of a centimeter in size and live for the extraordinarily short time of 10 with 43 zeros of a second. A flash from your typical camera 'lasts 10 million billion billion billion billion times longer!'[6]

This is our God, your God. And to think that this God, instead of casting us aside into a well-deserved hell, has given himself to us for our contemplation and enjoyment and delight, to be our source, our strength, our rock, our hope, our friend ... forever!

So What?

Why all these scientific facts? Because I want you to have something to sing about on Sunday. I want you to have a reason not to sin on Monday. I want you to have grounds for confidence when all else in life crumbles in a heap at your feet. I want you to have something to fill your daydreams other than illicit sex or more money or some other mindless, meaningless fantasy. I want you to have reason to fear God, to tremble before this awesome, all-consuming fire to whom we must one day given an account of every word and deed. I want you to have something of substance to tell your non-Christian neighbor. People who serve a shrunken God have nothing to offer a world on the brink of hell.

These many descriptions of profound truth concerning the natural world are of immense practical benefit, for they are designed to arouse in us awe and amazement at our God and intense trembling of soul and spirit and mind and will. I devoted two chapters to this topic because I believe that knowing God changes lives.

Let me put it this way. Neither financial liquidity nor a diversified portfolio will ultimately sustain the soul through economic crisis. Sheer will-power can't energize the spirit of man to stand against the increased paganizing of our society. It isn't therapy or theories about human behavior that will ultimately infuse the heart with hope when terror and death engulf the earth. It isn't good intentions or psychological strategies or another set of New Year's resolutions that will ultimately empower weak people to say 'No' to the passing pleasures of sin. And it isn't new legislation or lower taxes or a president of either political party in the White House that will deepen our moral roots in the face of a global erosion of values and righteousness.

What we need is a heart that is strengthened and sustained by the knowledge and experience and love of a really, really, really, big and beautiful God!

How Great Thou Art!

In a world seemingly run amok, where terrorism prevails and once stable corporations collapse, we need to reinvigorate our hearts with a fresh vision of the magnitude and beauty of divine power. The testimony of God in his Word is unmistakable.

He is 'mighty in strength' (Job 9:4). Our God is 'the LORD strong and mighty' (Ps. 24:8). Bolster your confidence with the knowledge that 'the LORD your God is in your midst, a great and awesome God' (Deut. 7:21). He is 'the LORD of hosts, the Mighty One of Israel' (Isa. 1:24). Jeremiah celebrated divine sovereignty by declaring of God: You have made 'the heavens and the earth by your great power and by your outstretched arm. Nothing is too hard for you. You show steadfast love to thousands, but you repay the guilt of fathers to their children after them, O great and mighty God, whose name is the LORD of hosts, great in counsel and mighty in deed' (Jer. 32:17-19a). Creation is a living testimony to 'the greatness of his might' (Isa. 40:26). He is Lord, Owner, Ruler, and King of all creation, whom none can resist or overpower (Matt. 11:25; Rev. 1:8; Ps. 29:10; Jer. 10:7,10). He is 'the Lord Almighty' (2 Cor. 6:18; Rev. 4:8; 11:17), 'the blessed and only Sovereign, the King of kings and Lord of lords' (1 Tim. 6:15). Nothing is too difficult for him; all things are within his power (Gen. 18:14; Zech. 8:6; Jer. 32:27).

When Mary interrogated Gabriel how she, a virgin, could conceive a child without the involvement of a man, his response was that *'nothing will be impossible with God'* (Luke 1:37). After comparing the difficulty of a rich man getting into heaven with a camel passing through the eye of a needle, Jesus said: *'With man this is impossible, but with God all things are possible'* (Matthew 19:26).

Immerse your mind in these pointed declarations:

- *Our God is in the heavens; he does all that he pleases* (Ps. 115:3).
- *Whatever the LORD pleases, he does, in heaven and on earth, in the seas and all deeps* (Ps. 135:6).
- *For the Lord of hosts has purposed, and who will annul it? His hand is stretched out, and who will turn it back?* (Isa. 14:27).
- *I am God, and there is none like me, declaring the end from the beginning and from ancient times things not yet done, saying, 'My counsel shall stand, and I will accomplish all my purpose'* (Isa. 46:9,10).
- *Then Job answered the LORD and said: 'I know that you can do all things; and that no purpose of yours can be thwarted'* (Job 42:1-2).
- *All the inhabitants of the earth are accounted as nothing, and he does according to his will among the host of heaven and among the inhabitants of the earth; and none can stay his hand or say to him, 'What have you done?'* (Dan. 4:35).

We must never think that what God actually does is the limit of what he could do. God *can* do all he wills (and does) but *need not do all he can* (and does not). That is to say, God's infinite power is manifested in the works of creation, but isn't exhausted by them. God could have created more than he has, if he so pleased. What God *has* done, therefore, is no measure of what he *could* have done or can do.

So I ask, Does God have the power to break the stranglehold that sin has on our hearts? He does! Does God have the power to energize us to hang on and persevere when every fiber of our being cries out: Quit! Quit! Yes, he does! Does God have the power to defeat the devil and the tormenting taunts and accusations we continually hear? Yes, he does! Does God have the power to heal our inner wounds and the years of bitterness in our souls? Does he have the power to break the power of pornography in our minds? Can the revelation of his beauty replace the ugly and defiling images of perversion? Does he have the power to enable us to cope with an unbelieving spouse and a rebellious teenager? Yes, and again, yes, he does.

This is the point at which we should all put down our books and log off our computers and adore and honor and praise our God. Stephen Charnock put it best:

> *Wisdom and power are the ground of the respect we give to men; they being both infinite in God, are the foundation of a solemn honour to be returned to him by his creatures. If a man make a curious engine, we honour him for his skill; if another vanquish a vigorous enemy, we admire him for his strength; and shall not the efficacy of God's power in creation, government, redemption, inflame us with a sense of the honour of his name and perfections! We admire those princes that have vast empires, numerous armies, that have a power to conquer their enemies, and preserve their own people in peace; how much more ground have we to pay a mighty reverence to God, who, without trouble and weariness, made and manages this vast empire of the world by a word and beck! What sensible thoughts have we of the noise of thunder, the power of the sun, the storms of the sea! These things, that have no understanding, have struck men with such a reverence that many have adored them as gods. What reverence and adoration doth this mighty power, joined with an infinite wisdom in God, demand at our hands.[7]*

Wherein is Our Significance?

Not everyone is comforted by the things I've said in these last two chapters. After speaking at a church conference on this subject a lady approached me in obvious emotional pain. She was overwhelmed by my portrayal of the expanse of the universe and stunned by the description of how small are the building blocks of the material world. She already felt inconsequential, having been abandoned by her husband and ignored by the church. She was one lone life amidst six billion people, all of whom, she thought, had more to offer than she ever would.

Then she heard me speak. Given the indescribably tiny dimensions of our globe in comparison with the vast and immeasurable reach of the universe as a whole, she felt threatened with utter insignificance. 'I'm smaller than a pin-prick in the midst of infinite space,' she bemoaned. 'How can a God of such unfathomable majesty and greatness bring himself to care about me?'

All I could think to say was that this is the breathtaking reality of divine grace, that in this immense cosmos, amidst the colossal structures of creation, our triune God has focused all his infinite energy and love and passionate affection on, of all things, broken sinners like you and me. Though God's presence fills the galaxies billions of light years away, he has mercifully chosen to become one of us in the person of Jesus. When I think that this God-man then yielded his life on a cruel cross that we might enjoy his glorious presence forever, I tremble. But our ultimate significance does not come from his having elevated us from the pit of guilt and shame, but in his graciously enabling us to enjoy endlessly elevating him. There is no greater honor or higher value than that found in the soul's ineffable delight in making much of so gracious and kind and beautiful a God as he.

[1] Maybe this will help. Bryson points out that 'protons are so small that a little dib of ink like the dot on this 'i' can hold something in the region of 500,000,000,000 of them, rather more than the number of seconds contained in half a million years' (*A Short History*, p. 9).

[2] Brian Greene, *The Elegant Universe: Superstrings, Hidden Dimensions, and the Quest for the Ultimate Theory* (New York: W. W. Norton & Company, 1999), p. 18.

[3] Trinh Xuan Thuan, *Chaos and Harmony: Perspectives on Scientific Revolutions of the Twentieth Century*, translated by Axel Reisinger (New York: Oxford University Press, 2001), p. 166.

[4] Greene, *The Elegant Universe*, p. 264.

[5] Thuan, *Chaos and Harmony*, pp. 183-84.

[6] Ibid., p. 184.

[7] Stephen Charnock, *The Existence and Attributes of God* (Grand Rapids: Sovereign Grace, 1971), p. 429.

Chapter Seven
Sweeter than all Pleasure

It is a dreary holiness indeed that is merely resisting sin. The joy of holiness is found in having heard a sweeter song.

So, what difference does it make? What's the practical payoff? How does our Christian Theory of Everything translate into power when we're in a face-off with sin? When temptation comes knocking, what good is grandiose talk of beauty and splendor and the God of quarks and quasars?

The answer is found in a story that could change your life. It's about one mysterious island, two heroic men, and a host of 'women' whose beauty was quite literally skin-deep. But mostly it's about radically different perspectives on the nature of Christianity and living to the glory of God.

I've shared this story countless times in churches and conferences both in America and abroad and wrote about it in my book *Pleasures Evermore*.[1] Wherever I go people plead with me to tell it again. Others comment on how powerfully it touched them or challenged their false notions of the Christian life. Don't be put off by the fact that it comes from Greek mythology. The point it makes is thoroughly biblical.

The first of our two characters is well known to most. Some call him Odysseus, others Ulysses. When I hear his name I close my eyes and envision the craggy features and dimpled chin of Kirk Douglas, the actor who portrayed him in the film version of our story. In a 1997 remake of the classic tale Armand Assante played the leading role. Ulysses was a devoted husband to his wife, Penelope, adored his son, and agonized at leaving his home of Ithaca. But he was also a Greek, and duty called.

Paris, the prince of Troy, had stolen away Helen, the woman 'whose face launched a thousand ships'. She was the wife of Menelaus, the King of Greece. He, together with his brother Agamemnon, Ulysses, and a mighty Greek army undertook the daunting task of recapturing her and restoring dignity to their beloved land.

To make a long story short, hidden in the belly of a huge Trojan horse, Ulysses and his men gained access to the city, slaughtered its inhabitants, and rescued the captive Helen. But the return voyage to Ithaca, which lasted nearly a decade, would prove to be far more challenging.

People are intrigued by Ulysses' encounter with the witch Circe and his careful navigation between the treacherous Scylla and Charybdis. Hollywood has done an admirable job of portraying for us the adventures of our Greek hero. And who can forget his blinding of the Cyclops Polyphemus, son of Poseidon, god of the seas?

My fascination, however, has always been with the infamous Sirens. Countless were the unwitting sailors who, on passing by their island, succumbed to the outward beauty of the Sirens and their seductively irresistible songs. Once lured close to shore, their boats crashed on the hidden rocks lurking beneath the surface of the sea. These demonic cannibals whose alluring disguise and mesmerizing melodies had drawn them close wasted little time in savagely consuming their flesh.

Ulysses had been repeatedly warned about the Sirens and their lethal hypocrisy. Upon reaching their island, he ordered his crew to put wax in their ears lest they be lured to their ultimate demise. He commanded them to look neither to the left nor right but to row for their lives. Ulysses had other plans for himself. He instructed his men to strap him to the mast of the ship, leaving his ears unplugged. 'I want to hear their song. No matter what I say or do, don't untie me until we are safely at a distance from the island.'

The songs of the Sirens were more than Ulysses' otherwise strong will could resist. He was utterly seduced by their sound and mesmerized by the promise of immediate gratification. One Siren even took on the form of Penelope, Ulysses' wife, seeking to lure him closer on the delusion that he had finally arrived home. Were it not for the ropes that held him tightly to the mast, Ulysses would have succumbed to their invitation. Although his hands were restrained, his heart was captivated by their beauty. Although his soul said 'Yes', the ropes prevented his indulgence. *His no was not the fruit of a spontaneous revulsion but the product of an external shackle.*

Ulysses' encounter with the Sirens, together with his strategy for resisting their appeal, is all too similar to the way many Christians try to live as followers of Jesus Christ. Like him, their hearts pant for the passing pleasures of sin. Their wills are no match for the magnetic power of sensual indulgence. Although they understand what is at stake, they struggle through life saying no to sin, not because their souls are ill-disposed to evil but because their hands have been shackled by the laws and rules imposed by an oppressive religious atmosphere. It is the extra-biblical taboo that comes thundering from a legalistic pulpit or a long-standing denominational prohibition that accounts for their external complicity. *Their obedience is not the glad product of a transformed nature but a reluctant conformity born of fear and shame.*

I have no desire to live that way. Neither do you, I suspect. So, how do you account for your 'obedience'? Is it the expression of your deepest heart-felt joy? Is it the product of a passion that spontaneously and urgently springs from the depths of your being? Or are you firmly bound to the mast of religious expectations, all the while yearning for the opposite of what you actually do? What is the most effective scheme for confronting the sinful sounds of Sirens?

A Sweeter Song

Jason, like Ulysses, was himself a character of ancient mythology, perhaps best known for his pursuit of the famous Golden Fleece. Again, like Ulysses, he faced the temptation posed by the sonorous tones of the Sirens. But his solution was of a different sort. Jason brought with him on the treacherous journey a man named Orpheus, the son of Oeager. Orpheus was a musician of incomparable talent, especially on the lyre and flute. When his music filled the air it had an enchanting effect on all who heard. There was not a lovelier or more melodious sound in all the ancient world.

When it came time, Jason declined to plug the ears of his crew. Neither did he strap himself to the mast to restrain his otherwise lustful yearning for whatever pleasures the Sirens might offer. But this was not the reckless decision of an arrogant heart. Jason had no illusions about the strength of his will or his capacity to be deceived. He was no less determined than Ulysses to resist the temptations of the Sirens. But he chose a different strategy.

He ordered Orpheus to play his most beautiful and alluring songs. The Sirens didn't stand a chance! Notwithstanding their collective allure, Jason and his men paid no heed to the Sirens. They were not in the least inclined to succumb. Why? Was it that the Sirens had ceased to sing? Was it that they had lost their capacity to entice the human heart? Not at all. Jason and his men said 'No' because *they were captivated by a transcendent sound.* The music of Orpheus was of an altogether different and exalted nature. Jason and his men said No to the sounds of the Sirens because they had heard something far more sublime. They had tasted something far sweeter. They had encountered something far more noble.

For many people Christianity is a tedious and ultimately unsatisfying aversion to temptations they would much prefer to indulge. Nothing depresses me more than to think of expending my one life on earth merely suppressing my deepest desires, always acting contrary to what my soul continues to crave. But there is little hope of it being otherwise so long as I seek satisfaction in something other than God.

Here's my point, both in this story and in the book as a whole. I don't want simply to live the Christian life. I want to *love* living the Christian life. Ulysses may have *survived* the sounds of Sirens. But only Jason *triumphed* over them. Yes, both men 'obeyed' (in a manner of speaking). Neither succumbed. Neither indulged his desires. Both men escaped the danger at hand. But only one was *changed*.

That's why you're reading this book. You want to change. Change 'out of' and 'into' what, only you know. But there is in your heart a chronic ache to be different, to be other than you are, to become what you haven't been. Life is all about transformation of one sort or another. The poor want to be wealthy. The feeble want to be healed. The overweight yearn to shed pounds. The middle-aged are terrified of liver spots and sagging skin. Depressed people only wonder what happiness feels like. The lonely long for friendship and the enslaved dream of freedom. Everyone is either in process of change or resisting its pressure or lamenting its absence.

For many Christians, it's often the latter. They're burdened by guilt, paralyzed by fear, in bondage to lust, eaten up with envy, and worst of all, bored stiff. They know that Jesus spoke of 'abundant life' (John 10:10) and Peter said something about 'joy that is inexpressible and filled with glory' (1 Pet. 1:8). But such words strike, at best, a distant chord. They examine their souls and are horrified at what they find: selfishness and greed and pride and unforgiveness. I won't make it any more painful by extending the list.

That's why you're *still* reading this book. What drives you is more than curiosity. You're wondering if perhaps something will be said that might make things different. Little else has worked. Not that we haven't tried. Oh, how we've tried— sanctified therapies, five-step formulas, deliverance, counseling. If self-denial fails, we try self-assertion. If self-sacrifice fails, we turn to self-indulgence. Many are beginning to feel hopeless. But I do have a suggestion. Here it is.

The essence of loving living as a follower of Jesus isn't in trying harder but in enjoying more. I'm not saying you can change without trying. I'm saying that enjoyment empowers effort. Pleasure in God is the power for purity.

The vice-grip the pleasure of sin exerts on the human soul will be broken only by trusting God's promise of superior pleasure in knowing Jesus. The only way to conquer one pleasure is with another, greater and more pleasing pleasure. Whether it's the sound of Sirens in ancient mythology or the all-too-real appeal of contemporary society, the principle is the same. *Our only hope is in maximizing our pleasure in God.*

These are the options. Like Ulysses, you can continue to fight against the restrictive influence of religious ropes and the binding power of fear, reprisal, and guilt, while your heart persists in yearning for what your hand is denied, or, like Jason, you can shout a spontaneous and heartfelt 'No!' to the sounds of Sirens because you've heard a sweeter sound! Either you devote your time and energy to demonstrate the ugliness and futility of sin and the world, hoping that such will embolden your heart to say no to it, as unworthy of your affection, or you demonstrate the beauty and splendor of all that God is for you in Jesus and *become happily and joyfully enticed by a rival affection.*

There are, I believe, only two kinds of Christians: those *driven* by fear and uncertainty, on the one hand, and those *drawn* by fascination and joy on the other. The former motivate themselves to 'obey' with the constant reminder of the dreadful consequences of failure or the shameful humiliation of 'getting caught'. It is more the terrifying prospect of public exposure than the allure of heavenly joy that accounts for how they live.

The others aren't immune to the promptings of the flesh. They know how appealing the world can be. But their hearts are energized by the incomparable attraction of divine beauty. Their wills are empowered not by the expectations of ecclesiastical authorities but by the enjoyment that flows from having encountered the glory of God in the face of Jesus Christ. 'True saints,' says Gerald McDermott, 'do what they do because they are drawn by love. True Christians find that the love of God in Christ is so attractive, so beautiful, that they cannot help *wanting* to serve him. There is a splendor, a beauty, about God and his ways that *lures* human beings to him.'[2]

To put it simply, the only way to liberate the heart from servitude to the passing pleasure of sin is by cultivating a passion for the joy and delight of beholding the beauty of Jesus. We must solidify in our souls the unshakeable confidence that we were fashioned by God for nothing less. What elevates the human soul and empowers it to live in the fullness of its created purpose is not religious intimidation or new rules or an anxiety induced by spiritual scoldings. It is faith in the promise that the enjoyment sin brings is fleeting and futile, but at God's right hand, and in the presence of his radiant glory, are pleasures evermore (Ps. 16:11).

A Window on the World

If you want to know what makes people tick, pick up any newspaper, weekly magazine, or force yourself to endure one day of *Oprah, Jerry Springer,* and *'E'.* I have too much self-respect to expose myself to the latter three so I narrowed it down to the 28 May 2002, edition of *USA Today* and the 3 June 2002 issue of *Newsweek,* both of which appeared in my mail box on the same day. Consider the following representative items.

• The first thing I noticed was the all too familiar story of yet another suicide bomber, an Islamic extremist who blew himself up at a shopping mall outside Tel Aviv. Ostensibly on the deluded assumption that he would gain immediate access to heaven and be rewarded with unending sensual pleasures, he happily killed a baby girl, a woman, and injured forty others.

• Moving from the horrific to the absurd, the paper reported that U.S. consumers spent $15.4 billion on athletic footwear in 2001. You read it right. Not $15 million but $15 *billion!*

• On a somewhat related note there was a story about the popularity of what has come to be known as X Games which includes sports such as skateboarding, bicycle stunt riding, freestyle motocross jumping and inline skating. Evidently the danger of such activities accounts for their widespread appeal.

• On the lighter and somewhat frivolous side, the movie *Spider Man* by this date had grossed $334 million (in its first twenty-five days of release) and *Star Wars, Episode II: Attack of the Clones* reached $200 million in only twelve days.

• An article in *Newsweek* reported on 'The "Sextasy" Craze' in which men are ingesting a mixture of the drug ecstasy and Viagra, the now famous pill designed to treat erectile dysfunction.

• At the bottom of the same page was the tragic account of a thirteen-year-old altar girl's journey into cyber-space. She exchanged messages with several men in chat rooms and often met them later for sex. One such man strangled her to death and dumped her body in a ravine.

• Then there was a sidebar extolling the virtues of 'Airplane Yoga' designed after 9/11 to help nervous passengers relax while in flight.

• Finally, the *Newsweek* lead article concerned the trials and triumphs of teenage girls and the ever-elusive goal of 'popularity'. One girl summed it up best when asked if it would be hard not to be popular: 'If I was cut off from all that? If you made me homely looking? And gave me [only] three friends? And made me study all the time? I'd probably shoot myself' ('Meet the Gamma Girls' by Susannah Meadows, p. 44).

Tomorrow's news won't be much different, perhaps only more salacious and extreme. Random information, you say? Meaningless drivel? Perhaps. But I suspect there is more to it than that. Could it be a testimony to what the Bible tells us about human nature and our passion for excitement? Might it be a curious-but-sad expression of humanity's relentless pursuit of pleasure, whether in the warped sense of personal value one derives from killing one's enemies as an act of religious devotion or the rush of a drug-induced sexual high or the thrill of being 'liked' or 'feared' by one's peers and the extremes to which one will go to make it happen?

Some might read these news items and laugh aloud at the dizzying variety of mindless antics people pursue in their desire for fulfillment. My response moved from stunned disbelief to a sadness bordering on despondency. How tragic, I thought, to see men and women who were created for transcendent and everlasting joy squandering their time, health, money, and energy grasping at wind, hoping for a momentary thrill when God offers them an eternity of indescribable pleasure.

I suppose some who read these stories found them strangely appealing, although they might be hesitant to admit it. They felt something come alive in their souls. Perhaps they caught sight of a glimmer of hope of being set free from the terminal boredom that dominates their lives. After all, if such behavior didn't work, at least in the short term, no one would bother with it.

So, how do we live in a world that encourages and endorses so many temptations? The promise of immediate gratification, often at a cut-rate price, is everywhere. Anonymous thrills. Self-affirming self-indulgence. And it seems to deliver.

People who say they love God often react in one of three ways. Some choose to isolate themselves from the world. Stay home, pull down the shades, and for heaven's sake don't turn on the TV. Others indulge themselves in the world, yielding to the pressure for the promise of a momentary joy-ride. Then there are the ones, the majority, I suspect, who scold themselves into slavish self-denial and call it holiness.

There's a better way.

Born in Darkness

Everyone, whether Catholic or Protestant, has heard of St. Augustine. Not all are aware, however, that there was a time when he was anything but a saint! More important still, I can't think of a better example of someone who discovered the life-changing power of delight in God.

He was born on 13 November 354, in the small North African city of Thagaste. He died on 28 August 430. His father, Patricius, was a pagan who reportedly professed faith in Christ and was baptized just before his death in 370. Augustine's relationship with his father was less than ideal. He was incredibly lax when it came to discipline and permitted his son to do pretty much as he pleased. Augustine had an older brother (Navigius) and a sister whose name he never mentioned.

Augustine's mother, Monica, was a devout Christian who prayed for her son without fail. Her intercession was fueled by a dream in which she saw herself and her son walking hand-in-hand in heaven. At eleven Augustine was sent to Madaura, twenty miles south of Thagaste, where he was trained in the classical poets and orators as well as Latin grammar. He stayed in Madaura until he was sixteen.

By his own confession, Augustine was a wild and lawless youth. He stole simply for the pleasure of stealing and excelled at lying. Notwithstanding his father's lack of involvement, Augustine didn't escape harsh discipline. 'He was thrashed repeatedly in school, for impudence and for playing dice and bones in class. Years later when he was an old man and wore the miter of a bishop, the memory of those thrashings remained vivid in his mind; he would conjure up in an agony of remorse the stripes on the bleeding flesh.'[3]

When he turned eighteen he was sent to Carthage in North Africa where he soon became chief in the school of rhetoric.

Before he arrived there his mother had given him a warning:

> *My mother commanded me not to commit fornication,
> and especially that I should not defile any man's wife. This
> seemed to me no better than women's counsels, which it
> would be a shame for me to follow. ... I ran headlong with
> such blindness that I was ashamed among my equals to be
> guilty of less impudence than they were, whom I heard brag
> mightily of their naughtiness; yea, and so much the more
> boasting by how much more they had been beastly; and I
> took pleasure to do it, not for the pleasure of the act only,
> but for the praise of it also.*[4]

He defiantly obtained a mistress, with whom he lived for
many years, who also bore him his only child, a son named
Adeodatus (lit., 'gift of God'). Augustine became engrossed in
the theater and the imaginary joys and sorrows of its actors. He
was set free from this fantasy world when he was introduced to
philosophy through the reading of Cicero's *Hortensius*. He was
soon enamored with Manichaeism, a form of Gnostic
philosophy that espoused a radical form of *metaphysical
dualism*. The Manichaeans believed that good and evil were
both eternal, co-equal in power, and engaged in unending conflict
with the outcome uncertain. Augustine remained a Manichaeist
for nine years, after which he settled in Milan, Italy, to resume
his teaching career.

Born Again in Light

While in Milan, Augustine came under the influence of its
intelligent and articulate bishop, Ambrose. However, if there
was a decisive human factor in his ultimate conversion, it was
his mother Monica and her undying intercession. She 'shed more
tears [over] my spiritual death,' said Augustine, 'than other

mothers shed for the bodily death of a son.'[5] Once, when Monica sought the advice of an aged bishop, she was told: 'Leave him alone. Just pray to God for him. From his own reading he will discover his mistakes and the depth of his profanity. … Leave me and go in peace. It cannot be that the son of these tears should be lost.'[6]

The major obstacle in Augustine's life was not intellectual but moral: he had lived with his mistress for fifteen years. One of his prayers was: 'Grant me chastity and continence, but not yet!' There is some disagreement about the extent of his sexual activity. He often spoke of how lust stormed confusedly within his soul, whirling him over the precipice of desire into a torrent of fornication that tossed and swelled and boiled and ran over. In one place he lamented the fact that he

> …cared nothing but to love and be loved. But my love went beyond the affection of one mind for another, beyond the arc of the bright beam of friendship. Bodily desire, like a morass, and adolescent sex welling up within me exuded mists which clouded over and obscured my heart, so that I could not distinguish the clear light of true love from the murk of lust.[7]

On the other hand, Garry Wills has recently argued that he was sexually faithful to his mistress. I lived 'with her alone,' he declared, and 'kept faith with her bed.' After he ended the relationship, 'he took a 'stopgap' mistress to tide him over until the marriage. It is characteristic that he did not resort to promiscuity, but to another sole concubine.'[8]

Notwithstanding his struggle, the Lord graciously sought him out and, in a manner of speaking, cornered him in a small garden attached to the house where he lived:

I now found myself driven by the tumult in my breast to take refuge in this garden, where no one could interrupt that fierce struggle in which I was my own contestant. ... I was beside myself with madness that would bring me sanity. I was dying a death that would bring me life.... I was frantic, overcome by violent anger with myself for not accepting your will and entering into your covenant. ... I tore my hair and hammered forehead with my fists; I locked my fingers and hugged my knees.[9]

Finally, while praying, he relates uttering these words: 'How long, how long? Tomorrow and tomorrow? Why not now? Why is there not this hour an end to my uncleanness?' Then came the miracle of saving grace:

I was saying these things and weeping in the most bitter contrition of my heart, when lo, I heard the voice as of a boy or girl, I know not which, coming from a neighbouring house, chanting, and oft repeating: 'Take up and read; take up and read' [tolle lege; tolle lege]. *I grasped the Bible, opened, and in silence read that paragraph on which my eyes first fell: 'not in rioting and drunkenness, not in chambering and wantonness, not in strife and envying; but put ye on the Lord Jesus, and make no provision for the flesh, to fulfill the lusts thereof.' No further would I read, nor did I need; for instantly, as the sentence ended – by a light, as it were, of security into my heart – all the gloom of doubt vanished away.[10]*

His resistance was overcome by 'sovereign joy', the name he gave to divine grace. He writes:

How sweet all at once it was for me to be rid of those fruitless joys which I had once feared to lose! ... You drove

*them from me and took their place, you who are sweeter
than all pleasure. ... O Lord my God, my Light, my Wealth,
and my Salvation.*[11]

As I said earlier, some statements have the power to change
lives. If I hadn't already given pride of place to the declaration
by Jonathan Edwards, this utterance by Augustine would top
my list. The good news is, I really don't need to choose, for
they're saying the same thing. It's all about the transformation
and exhilaration of the soul through the power of enjoying
God.

Fruitless Joys

Whatever failure or frustration you've experienced in life is
directly related to the degree to which you have given your heart
to fruitless joys. What an interesting choice of words: 'fruitless
joys'. What are they? Why did Augustine describe his life in
these terms?

Fruitless joys are what we turn to when life is boring and
gray and lonely and we know that tomorrow nothing will have
changed. Fruitless joys aren't necessarily scandalous sins. They
may be little more than harmless hobbies in which we invest
countless hours to make life a little less dull. They may be the
newest gadgets we work so hard to own and worry about losing.
They may be the fantasies and daydreams that swirl around in
our heads that we know will never come true but somehow
strangely bring a measure of excitement to an otherwise dreary
life.

Fruitless joys vary from person to person. For one, it may be
lingering bitterness of heart against someone who betrayed them.
For another, disillusionment with how life has turned out. For
another, anger and unforgiveness that energize the soul in a
perverse sort of way. Fruitless joys can be anything from the

mental escape that comes from identifying with the life of a Hollywood actress to the sheer excitement of new gossip. Or it may be something more serious such as internet pornography or cheating on your taxes or pride or infidelity or alcohol or drugs or whatever it is, as Augustine said, that you're convinced you can't live without, something without which life can't be faced. For Augustine, it was something he once 'feared to lose'.

For some it's not just the fear of loss. They're convinced they *deserve* them. 'If you only knew how many times people let me down. God too. If you only knew how much I've had to put up with, you'd ease up and concede me a few fruitless joys!'

But why call them 'fruitless' joys? If you think about it, it's obvious. They are fruitless because no matter how effective they seem right now, in the long term they can't satisfy. Often they leave us feeling guilty for our having squandered so much time and energy and money on something so trivial and petty. They lack the capacity to go beyond surface impact. They fail to reach deep into the soul and make a difference where it counts. They leave us empty and wondering aloud, 'There's got to be more to living than *this*.' Fruitless joys are whatever we trust to bring change but prove powerless to help us in our battle with temptation. No matter how well they work in the immediate present, we know God made us for something bigger and better and more satisfying.

So why do we hold on to them so vigorously? Why do we live in constant fear that they might be taken from us? Because they are fruitless 'joys'. No matter how fleeting or transient or ultimately unsatisfying they may be, they are, nonetheless, *joys*. Augustine didn't speak of fruitless 'events' or fruitless 'things' but of fruitless 'joys'. We continually revert to them in times of boredom and distress because they work! At least, for the moment they do.

Consider what this tells us about the nature of our souls. Your heart will always be drawn to whatever brings it greatest joy. Don't apologize for it. This isn't the result of poor nurture or genetic error or inadequate education. Far less is it the fruit of sin. God created you with a 'joy meter' in your soul, such that you invariably choose whatever options in life register most loudly and most deeply. You may be emotionally bruised, perhaps black and blue, from beating up on yourself for wanting to feel good or for wanting to experience happiness and joy. Stop it! Don't repent.

Augustine was convinced that if not philosophy then fornication, and if not fornication then the fantasies of the theater would bring him optimum, maximum joy. That's why he was so terrified of losing the 'fruitless joys' on which he had relied his whole life, ... until he met Jesus Christ. When by grace he tasted the goodness of God, the sweetness of salvation, those joys that had so long held his heart captive turned sour in his soul and became bitter to the taste and a stench in his nostrils.

Fruitless joys don't just magically disappear. They don't go away of their own accord. If their power to please begins to wane, the human soul will soon find adequate replacements. If Augustine, in describing his conversion and Christian life, had stopped upon saying, 'You [God] drove them from me,' other fruitless joys would quickly have been found to take the place of those he had forsaken.

Fruitless joys don't transmute of their own accord into pain and discomfort and ugliness. They will lose their grip on your soul only when they are displaced by greater joys, more pleasing joys, joys that satisfy not for the moment but forever. That is why Augustine declared, 'You [God] drove them from me and *took their place, you who are sweeter than all pleasure!*' Augustine didn't cease his sinful indulgence because he had given up on pleasure. He simply found a more pleasing pleasure, a longer-lasting joy, a fullness of joy and pleasures that never end (Ps. 16:11). By grace, his soul turned from reliance on fruitless joys to reliance on God's promise of a superior delight in his Son, Jesus Christ.

This is the true meaning of grace. Grace does not demonize our desires nor destroy them nor lead us to deny them. Grace is the work of the Holy Spirit in transforming our desires so that knowing Jesus becomes sweeter than illicit sex, sweeter than money and what it can buy, sweeter than every fruitless joy. Grace is God satisfying our souls with his Son so that we're ruined for anything else!

Stunned Speechless

Augustine was by no means alone in his transforming encounter. Seven centuries later the greatest of all medieval theologians, Thomas Aquinas, bore witness to a similar experience.

Thomas Aquinas was born in 1225 at Roccasecca in Italy. His father was Count Landulf of Aquino (thus the name Aquinas). He joined the Dominican order of monks in 1242 against his family's wishes, who preferred that he become a Benedictine. His father sent his brothers to kidnap him in an attempt to 'deprogram' the young man. They even tried, unsuccessfully, to lure him into sin with a prostitute, thinking that he would then regard himself as unfit for the ministry! Aquinas was held captive by his family for two years, although they eventually reconciled with him and approved his decision. Upon his release he immediately returned to the order, and began his studies at the university in Paris. He spent a dozen years teaching in Italy until he was recalled to Paris in 1269. He encountered opposition there and in 1272 was sent to Naples to establish a Dominican school. He died two years later on March 7, 1274, not yet fifty years old.

Legend has it that shortly after his death, miracles began to occur near the place where his body was laid. Monks at the Cistercian abbey at Fosanova, where Thomas was buried, feared that some might steal the body. They exhumed the corpse and cut off its head, placing the latter in a secret corner of the chapel. Mutilations continued for almost fifty years until all that remained were the bones. These were finally moved to the Dominican monastery at Toulouse where they remain to this day.

His teacher, Albert Magnus (Albert the Great) is alleged to have said of Aquinas: 'We call this lad a dumb ox, but I tell you that the whole world is going to hear his bellowing.' The nickname ('dumb ox') stayed with him throughout life. His two most notable works are the multivolume *Summa contra Gentiles* (a defense of Christianity against Muslim scholars in Spain and North Africa) and *Summa Theologica* (his systematic theology, regarded by some as the most ambitious and most rational book of theology ever written).

Aquinas was canonized as a saint in 1323 and given the title Angelic Doctor. Pope Pius V gave him the title Universal Doctor of the Church in 1567 during the Council of Trent (during the council a copy of the *Summa Theologica* was placed on the altar, second in importance only to the Bible). In all, he wrote more than 10,000,000 words in some sixty works! All of which I tell you to make this one simple point.

Lest one regard Thomas as a coldly intellectual theologian, devoid of godly passion, consider the story told of him by one young man. During his final years at Naples, Thomas was working on the conclusion of the *Summa* (which he never concluded!). A young man entered the room to find Thomas deep in prayer, allegedly floating above the ground. A voice was heard coming from the crucifix which Thomas held in hand: 'Thomas, you have written well of me. What reward can I give you for all your labors?' To which Thomas replied: 'Nothing, Lord. Nothing, but You.' Some time later, on 6 December 1273, he had an experience during Mass that so profoundly affected him that he wrote nothing more. When urged by his friends to complete the Summa, he replied: 'I cannot, for compared with what I have seen and what has been revealed to me [evidently, during the Mass], everything I have written seems like straw.'

Historians have speculated endlessly on what Thomas saw or heard or felt. We will never know for sure, but it must have been a revelation of divine glory so grand, a manifestation of spiritual beauty so breathtaking. that it put to shame the 10,000,000 words of theology Thomas had spent a lifetime writing.

Enjoying More

Augustine and Thomas both bear witness to the fact that there is a point at which knowledge serves its end and the human heart melts in stunned adoration. As I said before, the solution to our struggle with fruitless joys is not to try harder but to enjoy more! Enjoyment empowers effort. Doing is the fruit of delighting. Performance is energized by pleasure. God invites us to abandon fruitless joys so that we might taste the sweetness of salvation and hear the symphony of Christ's love and see the beauty of the Father's glory and feel the joy of his presence and smell the fragrance of his eternal goodness. This is what our souls were made for. And in this is God most glorified.

---

[1] Sam Storms, *Pleasures Evermore: The Life-Changing Power of Enjoying God* (Colorado Springs: NavPress, 2000), pp. 104-06.

[2] Gerald R. McDermott, *Seeing God: Twelve Reliable Signs of True Spirituality* (Downers Grove: IVP, 1995), p. 114.

[3] Robert Payne, 'The Dark Heart Filled with Light,' *Christian History*, Issue 67 (Vol. XIX, No. 3), pp. 12-13.

[4] Quoted by Payne, pp. 13-14.

[5] *The Confessions of St. Augustine*, translated with an introduction and notes by John K. Ryan (New York: Image Books, 1960), 3.11.

[6] Ibid., 3.12.

[7] *Confessions*, 2.2.

[8] Garry Wills, *Saint Augustine* (New York: Penguin Putnam, Inc. 1999), p. 41.

[9] *Confessions*, 8.8.

[10] *Confessions*, 8.12.

[11] *Confessions*, 9.1.

Chapter Eight
Dazzled by the Divine

On the glorious splendor of your majesty, and on your wondrous works, I will meditate.'

Psalm 145:5

I am rarely comfortable when left to guess at people's motives. I find it easier to listen to them speak, or read their words when they've come clean about their intentions. That's one of the things that draws me to the apostle Paul. He never leaves you perplexed about his purpose.

The church in first-century Corinth often questioned Paul's motivation, on occasion yielding to the temptation to accuse him of being self-serving and insensitive to their needs. Knowing this, Paul was careful in his second epistle to clarify precisely why he behaved as he did and why he was prepared to say the things he said. Read it carefully:

> But I call God to witness against me—it was to spare you that I refrained from coming again to Corinth. Not that we lord it over your faith, but we work with you for your joy, for you stand firm in your faith (2 Cor. 1:23-24).

I'm struck by how candid Paul is in declaring his conscious intent. Some in Corinth may have felt that Paul's behavior and frequent change of travel plans was indicative of an arrogant and authoritative style of leadership. But the apostle is quick to remind them that it was neither indifference to their needs nor pompous posturing that governed his actions. Rather, he made his decisions based on what he believed would best serve their *joy*! Paul had some harsh things to say to the Corinthians (deservedly so, I might add). His rebukes often stung. But his aim was always their *joy*! Paul didn't discharge his apostolic calling to expand his personal power or to broaden his influence or to bolster his reputation or to increase his control but *to intensify their joy in Jesus*.

Paul can almost be heard to say, 'Whether I'm rebuking you for sectarianism in the church (1 Corinthians 3) or laxity in moral conduct (1 Cor. 5–6) or abuse of spiritual power (1 Cor. 12–14), *my aim is your joy in Jesus*. Whether I appeal to you to be financially generous (2 Cor. 8–9) or warn you of false apostles (2 Cor. 11), *my aim is your joy in Jesus*.' Should Paul have been pressed for an explanation, I believe he would have answered like the good Christian hedonist that he was: 'because God is most glorified in you Corinthians (and all believers) when you are most pleased and satisfied and at rest in the plenitude of his beauty that can be seen in the face of Jesus Christ'.

Paul's commitment to their joy in Jesus was motivated, at least in part, by his belief that Satan was no less committed to their joy in the passing pleasures of sin (cf. Heb. 11:25). He knew all too well that the diabolical strategy of the enemy was to seduce them into believing that the world and the flesh and sinful self-indulgence could do for their weary and broken hearts what God couldn't. This is the battle that they and we face each day. We awaken to a world at war for the allegiance of our minds and the affections of our souls. The winner will be whoever can persuade us that he will bring greatest and most soul-satisfying joy. That is why Paul labored so passionately and sacrificially for joy in Jesus in the hearts of that first-century church. And that is also why I have written this book to the church of our day.

Thank God for Synonyms!

Enjoying God sounds good, but it needs substance. What exactly does it mean to 'relish and rejoice in Jesus'? When I first began to explore this question I experienced great frustration with the range of my vocabulary. Simply to speak of joy or delight or satisfaction struck me as hardly doing justice to the nature of our experience of God. There are intellectual and emotional dimensions to relishing God and rejoicing in the revelation of his glory that call for a variety of terms worthy of such an experience.

So I ransacked the dictionary looking for words that I hoped might elicit from your heart the response of spiritual intensity commensurate with the God whom we've been privileged to know. When the dictionary failed to deliver to my satisfaction, I turned to my thesaurus. In the few years that have passed since I began this effort I continue to sense the inadequacy of human language to articulate the joy for which we were fashioned.[1] But here's my best shot. This is what God intended when he created your heart and stamped his indelible image upon it. You were made to be

- enchanted ... enamored ... engrossed with God
- enthralled ... enraptured ... entranced with God
- enravished ... excited ... enticed with God
- astonished ... amazed ... awed with God

- astounded … absorbed … agog with God
- beguiled and bedazzled
- startled and staggered
- smitten and stunned
- stupified and spellbound
- charmed and consumed
- thrilled and thunderstruck
- obsessed and preoccupied
- intrigued and impassioned
- overwhelmed and overwrought
- gripped and rapt
- enthused, and electrified
- tantalized, mesmerized, and monopolized
- fascinated, captivated, intoxicated, infatuated, and exhilarated … with God!

I often try to envision what my life would be like if this were an accurate description of my relationship with God. I suspect I would find it much more difficult to sin than I now do. I imagine that reading the Bible would never be remotely boring. I trust that I would display an uncommon boldness and courage in sharing Christ with my unsaved neighbors. I believe I would be less enamored with the glamour of Hollywood and the allure of Wall Street and find that generosity for those in need would come far more easily than it does today. And I'm certain that my worship would be theologically precise, physically expressive, emotionally intense, and filled with passion, intimacy, and an extravagance like that of Mary's when she poured the alabaster vial of expensive perfume on the feet of Jesus.

What are the odds of a typical unbeliever using the above list of words to describe Christians on any given Sunday? Minimal, at best. And we're stumped why people scoff at the church and treat us with casual disdain! Something has to change. That's why I've written this book. But my writing and your reading it are hardly adequate to turn the tide. Antecedent to all human effort and as a prelude to any enjoyment of God is the activity of God himself.

What is God Up To?

I believe, as I trust you do, that if Christianity is going to change, God's people must experience a deep, inner transformation beyond the external makeover that we so often pass off as spirituality. And if God's people are going to change, God himself must take steps to kindle afresh in our hearts the flame of fascination with his divine personality. Only God can awaken in our souls the marvel and wonder of which he is worthy. God must restore in his people the mystery and excitement of the knowledge of all that he is for us in Jesus. That alone will break the power of sin, deliver us from spiritual mediocrity, and bring us into the depths of delight for which he created us.

This book is dedicated to Mike Bickle who, on any number of occasions, has been heard to say: 'It takes God to love God.' Mike's point is that *loving God requires a loving God*. We will be passionate for him only so far as he is passionate for us. To love God as we were made to love him requires an antecedent love in God for those whom he has made. He must take the initiative. He must reveal the depths and extent of his commitment to us and the delight in his heart for broken people. Only then will our slumbering and self-centered souls be aroused to seek him with all our hearts and relish the revelation of himself in the person of his Son, the man Christ Jesus.

Virtually everywhere I go these days, whether I'm speaking in a church or at a conference or at Wheaton College, I encounter the same question: 'What's God up to? Is there anything in particular that you see or discern about what God is doing today and what we might expect tomorrow?' For many people that question is a round about way of saying: 'Are we in the last days? Is Jesus coming back soon?' The question has taken on added urgency ever since 11 September 2001. By the way, the answer is: 'I have absolutely no idea when he's coming back, and nobody else does either, so don't believe them.'

Make no mistake: I'm not a prophet, but I *do* know what God's up to. I believe I have a bit of spiritual discernment about what God is doing today and what we might expect tomorrow, although it may not be as exciting as you might wish. There isn't the slightest doubt in my mind about it. You don't have to be prophetic or a theological genius to figure it out. Just read your Bible and open your eyes.

So, what is God up to? If I may again use the words of Mike Bickle: *God is in the business of restoring the first commandment to first place in the hearts of his people.* The first and greatest commandment was articulated by Jesus in response to the question posed him by a young lawyer. Listen to Matthew 22:36-38. '"Teacher, which is the great commandment in the Law?" And he said to him, "*You shall love the Lord your God with all your heart and with all your soul and with all your mind. This is the great and first commandment.*"'

There is a global awakening happening every moment of every day, and it's all God's doing. This is an awakening of the human heart into the fullness of what it was created to experience. It's an awakening to passion for God and unashamed, extravagant affection for Jesus. I have in mind something that transcends an awakening merely to obedience or service or reverential fear or evangelism or missions. This is an awakening to something far more foundational and far more crucial, out of which all these other essential Christian activities inevitably flow.

As I said above, God created you to be a lover of God, to enjoy him, to delight in him, to be enthralled and entranced with him, to be excited and exhilarated with the revelation of himself in Jesus. In other words, God created you for the first and greatest commandment, to be a lover of God. This, above all else, is your fundamental identity. And *that* is what God's up to. With a resolute determination that cannot be thwarted he is arousing and stirring and wooing and beckoning the hearts of his people into a passionate and intimate love affair with His Son, the Lord Jesus Christ.

God is the consummate romantic. He longs to draw us to himself, to the joy of that intimacy he alone is capable of providing. Not everyone is happy with this. Some are frightened. Others are threatened. It touches something deep down inside their souls that they'd just as soon leave dead and dormant. The call for vulnerability and honesty challenges the self-protective veneer with which they've covered over their lives.

In their book, *The Sacred Romance*, Brent Curtis and John Eldredge challenge us to acknowledge and embrace the reality of what God has put within. Instead of denying our desire for pleasure and intimacy, instead of indulging it in sensuality, we must celebrate how God has made us and find satisfaction in his presence. The sacred romance, they explain,

> ...calls to us every moment of our lives. It whispers to us on the wind, invites us through the laughter of good friends, reaches out to us through the touch of someone we love. We've heard it in our favorite music, sensed it at the birth of our first child, been drawn to it while watching the shimmer of a sunset on the ocean. It is even present in

times of great personal suffering—the illness of a child, the loss of a marriage, the death of a friend. Something calls to us through experiences like these and rouses an inconsolable longing deep within our heart, wakening in us a yearning for intimacy, beauty, and adventure. This longing is the most powerful part of any human personality. It fuels our search for meaning, for wholeness, for a sense of being truly alive. However we may describe this deep desire, it is the most important thing about us, our heart of hearts, the passion of our life. And the voice that calls to us in this place is none other than the voice of God.[2]

All of us are keenly aware how hard it is to love the Lord with all our mind, heart, soul, and strength. Every time we begin to fan the flame of passion for God life throws a bucket of cold water on us. Each time we feel ourselves inching closer to the heart of God another obstacle is thrown in our way, something that causes us to retreat or withdraw or perhaps even run from his presence. If we are ever confidently to run to him we must first be drawn by the irresistible radiance of his beauty. It rests with the sovereign initiative of God alone to make known the glory of his face. And that is precisely what he's doing.

His Nearness to Us, Our Dearness to Him

The most precious passage in all of Scripture to me is Psalm 16:11. Here David speaks of the presence of God and the inimitable pleasure and power that flood the soul of those who experience it. Knowing this ought to instill in us a ravenous hunger for intimacy with God. What surprises many is to discover the immense practical benefit of such desire.

I first saw this in something said by the author of the epistle to the Hebrews. In the opening verses of chapter 13 we are exhorted to love each other (v. 1), to be hospitable (v. 2), to be compassionate to the oppressed and needy (v. 3), to pursue sexual purity both inside and outside of marriage (v. 4), and perhaps most difficult of all, not to love money but to be content (v. 5). A formidable task indeed!

How can God possibly expect such behavior from people as self-absorbed as we? The answer, in verses 5b-6, is found in a promise that *God himself* makes to every one of us: *"'I will never leave you nor forsake you.'"* So we can confidently say *"The Lord is my helper, I will not fear; what can man do to me?'"*

Both of my daughters are grown and well-educated now, but I can still remember the struggle I had with them to avoid using double negatives. One of their favorites was: 'I'm not never going there again.' I'd gently(?) correct them: 'No honey, don't use a double negative. Say 'I'm not *ever* going there again.'' 'Whatever, I ain't doing it.' 'No, honey, *don't never* say ain't' (oops!). I trust you get the point. My reason for mentioning this is that a deliberate double negative is present in the Greek text of our passage. The statement is quite emphatic and could be literally translated, *'not not will I leave you, neither not not will I forsake you,'* or better still, *'I will never, by no means ever, leave you; neither will I ever, by no means ever, forsake you.'*

This is related to what we read in Romans 8:1 where Paul makes the astounding declaration that 'there is therefore now no condemnation for those who are in Christ Jesus.' When we think of the word 'condemnation' and all it entails: the loss of hope, fear of the future, uncertainty of today, shattered dreams, painful separation, etc., Paul's statement suddenly begins to echo and reverberate in our hearts with a power and force that makes it feel as if we're going to explode with joy, exuberance, and gratitude!

When we wed these two texts (Romans 8:1 and Hebrews 13:5-6) we discover that if you are in Christ Jesus, there is no valid reason why you should ever again experience fear or apprehension about your relationship with God or your eternal destiny. That doesn't mean you *won't* experience such fear. It does mean there is no valid reason why you *should*.

The Christian is not one who swings like a spiritual pendulum, as if forgiven one moment and condemned the next, only to be forgiven yet again, endlessly back and forth between God's redeeming grace and retributive wrath. Paul couldn't have been more explicit. The definition of a Christian is one who is not now nor ever shall be condemned: no condemnation! A believer may *feel* condemned. For that matter, an unbeliever may feel forgiven (even though he isn't)! But this is not an issue of subjective sensations or inner impressions. This is our eternal position in Christ, now and forever.

What that means, practically speaking, is that you and I never, by no means ever again, have any excuse for being afraid of what others can do to us. We never, by no means ever again, have to try to do something *alone* that we know God wants us to do. Why? Because God, our omnipotent helper, is always and forever with us.

Think about it: since God is really and truly forever and always right here with you, other people cannot control or shape or determine your life. Some of you hear this statement in Hebrews 13:6—'What can man do to me?' and you say: 'Good grief, are you kidding? They can do a *lot* to me! They can beat me up, rob me, slander me, sue me, even kill me!'

But our author knows that. He said it explicitly in Hebrews 10:32-34 and in 11:35-38. Look right here in our passage at verse 3! Our writer isn't stupid. He knows that people can do a lot of really bad things to us. So what could he possibly mean in verse 6? Why does the promise 'I will never leave you or forsake you' cause him to feel so confident in verse 6 that he can declare that no man can do him harm? There are at least three answers.

First, no human can do anything to separate you from the love of God (Rom. 8:35-37). Notwithstanding the worst imaginable physical torment or emotional distress or financial disaster, you and I are forever safe in the arms of God. Second, God is able to cause all things people do to us, even the bad things, to work together for our good (Rom. 8:28). This isn't to say that all things *are* good, but that God can orchestrate the evil into a symphony of glory. And third, God enables us to respond with everlasting joy to whatever they do, by reminding us that we have 'a better possession and an abiding one' (Heb. 10:34).

Although the promise of verses 5b-6 follows immediately on the exhortation not to love money, I believe our author intends for us to understand that this is how we fulfill all five exhortations! We *can* love each other because God is always with us as our helper. We *can* be hospitable to strangers because God is always with us as our helper. We *can* find the energy and resources to help the oppressed and needy because God is always with us as our helper. We *can* live in sexual purity because God is always with us to help us. And we *can* break the power of money over our lives because God is always with us to help.

Perhaps the hardest thing of all is the exhortation not to love money. Infatuation with what money can do for us comes easily. But if this promise is true, the way to be free from the love of money is to know and believe and be satisfied by the promise of God summed up in 'I will never leave you nor forsake you.' If God really means that, then I don't need to crave after money as the source of my security and identity and pleasure. I can find all that and more in the enjoyment of intimacy with the God who promises never to leave! The bondage to money and what it can do for us is only broken by believing that God can do far more. Money makes a promise. So does God. The question is: Whom will you believe?

Beauty of a Different Color

I once heard John Piper say that sin is not the choice of pleasure but the loss of it. Or again, to sin is not to choose pleasure but to lose pleasure. That can only be true if what we deny ourselves in order to sin has the capacity to please more than the sin itself. The strength of all sin, whether simple or scandalous, is the lie that God can't do what it can. But, and it grieves me to say this, it's a lie that often rings true. The visible odds aren't in God's favor. Fornication seems a lot more fun than sexual purity and self-indulgence feels better than feeding the poor. Pride invites less pain than humility and getting drunk with wine sounds more exciting than being filled with the Holy Spirit (Eph. 5:18).

That we should ever think in these terms or buy into the lie proves that something is horribly amiss in our understanding of God. Something is seriously askew in our experience of his beauty that, if not addressed, bodes ill for our capacity to obey him and love him and enjoy him. Once again, Jonathan Edwards nailed it:

There is very great delight the Christian enjoys in the sight he has of the glory and excellency of God. How many arts and contrivances have men to delight the eye of the body. Men take delight in the beholding of great cities, splendid buildings and stately palaces. And what delight is often taken in the beholding of a beautiful face. May we not well conclude that great delights may also be taken in pleasing the eye of the mind in seeing the most beautiful, the most glorious, the most wonderful Being in the world?[3]

The answer is Yes! That sort of true happiness and sin-killing spiritual delight arise from the sight or apprehension of him who is preeminently excellent.

The beauty of God has many facets, like a rare and exquisite diamond that captivates a young couple in search of a wedding ring. Their failure would be to look at the jewel from only one angle and thus deprive themselves of the joy in seeing its true value. It's no different in our study of God.

Perhaps you've heard someone described as being 'one-dimensional'. No one intends that as a compliment! It's a nice way of saying the person is boring, bland, and unappealing. Some people are all too easy to understand. Not because they're clear, but because they're shallow. What you see on the surface is all you get. There's little, if any, mystery to them. Their personality is uninspiring and fairly predictable. You always know what they think, how they feel, and what they'll do regardless of the circumstances. They're more than stable. They're static. Inert. Invariable.

Although God always thinks and acts in perfect harmony with his nature, his nature is infinitely complex. His personality is deep and rich and diverse and ultimately inexhaustible. Just when you've got him figured out, he'll surprise you (but always in a good way).

Until now I've spoken almost exclusively of enjoying God in the revelation of his love and glory and radiance and beauty. But God is no less righteous than compassionate, no less a God of wrath than a God of mercy, and these attributes, no less than the others, ought to evoke in us awe and breathless amazement.

Consider, for example, the experience of the prophet Habakkuk as described by him in 3:16-19 of his prophecy:

I hear, and my body trembles; my lips quiver at the sound; rottenness enters into my bones; my legs tremble beneath me. Yet I will quietly wait for the day of trouble to come upon people who invade us. Though the fig tree should not blossom, nor fruit be on the vines, the produce of the olive fail and the fields yield no food, the flock be cut off from the fold and there be no herd in the stalls, yet I will rejoice in the LORD; I will take joy in the God of my salvation. GOD, the Lord is my strength; he makes my feet like the deer's; he makes me tread on my high places.

The circumstances surrounding Habakkuk's experience were unusual, to say the least. Habakkuk prophesied to the southern kingdom of Judah. In 722 B.C., about a century before Habakkuk lived, the northing kingdom had been destroyed by the Assyrians. The situation in Judah wasn't much better. A vivid description is found in 2 Kings 21:1–22:2, which portrays the abominations that came into the land through the reign of Manasseh (696-641 B.C.).

Things didn't improve much in the next quarter century. Habakkuk's persistent prayer was for God to act ... in judgment! He pleaded with the Lord to deal with his rebellious and idolatrous people. When God finally answered the prophet's prayer, it wasn't in the way he had hoped. 'Yes,' said the Lord, 'I will punish my people. I will raise up against them the Chaldeans. Then I will judge the Chaldeans for their own iniquity.'

Habakkuk was floored! 'But Lord, I agree with you that your people are wicked. Yes, they need severe chastisement. But *the Chaldeans?* They're worse than we are!' Notwithstanding Habakkuk's perplexity at the answer to his prayers, God was determined to punish his wicked people by means of an even more wicked people, the dreaded Babylonians. Chapter 3, verses 16-19, is the record of Habakkuk's response to the impending invasion from the east.

What Habakkuk describes in verse 16 should not be dismissed as over dramatization or figurative language. There's no reason not to take his words as a literal portrayal of a physically convulsive experience. As the truth of his vision sank deeply into his soul, his body inescapably felt its presence. His solar plexus heaves. Dialogue with God gives way to an inexplicable and inarticulate quivering of the lips. All strength drains from his bones, as if rottenness set in. His knees buckle under the weight of God's awesome majesty.

All of this is the result of his having 'heard' something. Heard what? Simply put, God's answer to Habakkuk's question about what he intended to do about sin in Judah. It was the inevitable reality of divine judgment, the revelation of divine wrath against sin, that shook Habakkuk deep in his bones. The prophet is awestruck by a God who is so majestic and sovereign as to do things as he does. Perhaps Habakkuk also saw a vision or had some revelatory experience of the impending judgment (cf. 3:3-6,10-12). The effect was staggering.

'My inward parts trembled,' (NASB) is a reference to the lower abdomen, but here used figuratively for the innermost thoughts, feelings, intents, and passions of the human soul (see Prov. 20:27). The word 'trembled' is also used in Exodus 15:14; Deuteronomy 2:25; Job 37:1-2 and means to convulse, to be shaken to the depths of one's being. This is obviously more than mere 'butterflies' in the stomach! (See also Ps. 29:3-5,7-9; 96:7-9; 114:7.)

As if that were not enough, 'my lips quivered,' said the prophet. He struggled to speak. It wasn't from cold that they quivered but from fear and amazement at the revelation of the divine purpose!

He didn't know how else to describe what he felt but to say, 'rottenness enters into my bones,' an indication that there descended on him a feeling of decaying, of disintegrating weakness in the marrow of his being. And finally, 'my legs tremble beneath me,' perhaps more literally rendered, 'I experienced a trembling step beneath me.' This once proud and strong prophet faltered and struggled to keep his balance, an experience not unlike what we read about in Daniel 10:9-10; Revelation 1:17; and Luke 24:32.

But his *fear* didn't eliminate his *faith*. Notwithstanding the ravages of a divinely induced war (v. 17), his confidence and delight in God remained unshaken (vv. 18-19). As D. A. Carson has said, 'firm resolve this may be; grim resolution it is not. It is the resolution of one whose eyes have been opened to see where his delight should have been in the first place.'[4]

Like a female sheep, says Habakkuk, I shall mount with swift surefootedness to the heights of the mountain (cf. Ps. 18:33). Says Robertson:

> *Surefooted, untiring, bounding with energy, the Lord's people may expect to ascend the heights of victory, despite their many setbacks. The heights of the earth, the places of conquest and domain, shall be the ultimate possession of God's people. As spokesman for God's people in this song to be celebrated through the ages, the prophet displays the magnificence of a victorious faith. Even the most horrifying setbacks cannot break the confidence in ultimate victory.*[5]

Where does one find such strength? How might you and I tap in to the sin-breaking, faith-elevating, persevering power of Habakkuk and so many others like him? There are no shortcuts or secret solutions or magical five-step formulas that somehow didn't make their way into Scripture. *Becoming is the fruit of beholding* the beauty of our radiant and resplendent God as he has made himself known in his incarnate Son, Jesus Christ.

Oh God, Father of glory, grant us the Spirit of wisdom and revelation who brings the sin-killing knowledge of your Son, our Savior. As we dig deeply in your Word, enlighten the eyes of our hearts and enable us to see him in all his radiant glory. Be merciful and stir us from spiritual slumber that we might be energized by the knowledge of the hope to which you have called us. Oh Father, the world has anesthetized our souls to the greatness of your grace. Awaken us to the incomparable privilege that is ours of being your eternal inheritance and satisfy us fully and joyfully and generously with the beauty of your Son. Amen.

---

[1] My initial effort to communicate this truth is found in my book, *Pleasures Evermore* (NavPress, 2000).

[2] Brent Curtis and John Eldredge, *The Sacred Romance: Drawing Closer to the Heart of God* (Nashville, TN: Thomas Nelson, 1997), p. 195.

[3] Jonathan Edwards, 'The Pleasantness of Religion,' in *Sermons and Discourses, 1723-1729*, The Works of Jonathan Edwards, Volume 14. Edited by Kenneth P. Minkema (New Haven: Yale University Press, 1997), pp. 108-9.

[4] Donald A. Carson, *How Long, O Lord? Reflections on Suffering and Evil* (Grand Rapids: Baker Book House, 1990), pp. 76-77.

[5] O Palmer Robertson, *The Books of Nahum, Habakkuk, and Zephaniah* (Grand Rapids: Eerdmans, 1990), p. 247.

Chapter Nine
Joy's Eternal Increase

Labor to get a sense of the vanity of this world. ...
Labor to be much acquainted with heaven.'

Jonathan Edwards

To whatever degree we relish and rejoice in the beauty of God now, it is but a faint foretaste of the eternal feast we will enjoy in heaven in the age to come. Theologians and mystics often speak of this consummate experience of God's glory as the *beatific vision*, by which is meant an intuitive, unmediated, and unprecedented apprehension of the beauty of God (see Matthew 5:8; Revelation 22:4).

Not everyone thinks it helpful to focus on the future. They've bought into the old adage that people who do are 'so heavenly minded they're of no earthly good'. On the contrary, I'm persuaded that we will never be of much use in this life until we've developed a healthy obsession with the next. Our only hope for satisfaction of soul and joy of heart in this life comes from looking intently at what we can't see (see 2 Cor. 4:16-18;

Col. 3:1-4). Therefore, we must take steps to cultivate and intensify in our souls an ache for the beauty of the age to come.

The consistent witness of Scripture is that we should make heaven and its beauty the object of our contemplative energy, not for the purpose of fueling theological speculation but to equip us for life here and now. Evidently there is something about heaven that makes our anticipation of its experience profoundly life-changing. And the reason isn't hard to discern. *The essence of heaven is the vision of God and the eternal increase of joy in him.* Heaven might well be summed up in the declaration: *'They will see his face'* (Rev. 22:4)!

Why Think About Heaven?

Before I delve into the nature of this beatific vision, consider the immediate and practical impact of the soul's intense longing for it.

(1) A contemplative focus on the beauty of heaven frees us from excessive dependence upon earthly wealth and comfort. If there awaits us an eternal inheritance of immeasurable glory, it is senseless to expend effort and energy here, sacrificing so much time and money, to obtain for so brief a time in corruptible form what we will enjoy forever in consummate perfection.

Look closely at the context of Paul's words in Philippians 3:20-21. 'Our citizenship,'[1] says Paul, 'is in heaven' (3:20a). Knowing this enables the soul to escape the grip of 'earthly things' (Phil. 3:19) and to 'stand firm' (Phil. 4:1). Paul in no way denies or minimizes the reality of our earthly obligations. He reminds the Philippians that their bodies were in Philippi. Their names were enrolled as Roman citizens. They had voting rights. They owed their taxes to an earthly king. They were protected by the laws of a this-worldly state.

Yet their fundamental identity, the orientation of their souls, the affection of their hearts, and the focus of their minds was *in heaven*! Paul appeals to their patriotic pride, not in Philippi, but in the New Jerusalem, their real residence! Therefore be governed by *its* rules, *its* principles, *its* values. Paul is careful to insist that our citizenship 'is' (present tense) in heaven, not 'will be'. We are *already* citizens of a new state. We are resident aliens here on earth.

Peter contends that the ultimate purpose of the new birth (1 Pet. 1:3-4) is our experience of a *heavenly* hope, an inheritance that is 'imperishable,' by which he means incorruptible, not subject to decay or rust or mold or dissolution or disintegration. This heavenly inheritance is 'undefiled' or pure, unmixed, untainted by sin or evil. Best of all, it is 'unfading'. Not only will it never end, it will never diminish in its capacity to enthrall and fascinate and impart joy. It is 'reserved in heaven' for us, kept safe, under guard, protected and insulated against all intrusion or violation. This hope is the grounds for your joy (v. 6) that sustains you in trial and suffering.

A few verses later he exhorts his readers to 'set your hope fully on the grace that will be brought to you at the revelation of Jesus Christ' (1 Pet. 1:13). This is a commanded obsession. Fixate fully! Rivet your soul on the grace that you will receive when Christ returns. Tolerate no distractions. Entertain no diversions. Don't let your mind be swayed. Devote every ounce of mental and spiritual and emotional energy to concentrating and contemplating on the grace that is to come. What grace is that? It is the grace of the heavenly inheritance described in verses 3-6!

The expectation of a 'city that has foundations' energized Abraham's heart to persevere in a foreign land. All the patriarchs are described as 'seeking a [heavenly] homeland' (Hebrews

11:14). Their determination in the face of trial was fueled by their desire for a 'better country, that is, a heavenly one' (Hebrews 11:16). As pleasant as it may be now, what we see and sense and savor in this life is an ephemeral shadow compared with the substance of God himself. Earthly joys are fragmented beams, but God is the sun. Earthly refreshment is at best a sipping from intermittent springs, but God is the ocean!

(2) A contemplative focus on heaven enables us to respond appropriately to the injustices of this life. Essential to heavenly joy is witnessing the vindication of righteousness and the judgment of evil. Only from our anticipation of the new perspective of heaven, from which we, one day, will look back and evaluate what now seems senseless, can we be empowered to endure this world in all its ugliness and moral deformity.

Apart from a contemplative fixation on the glories of heaven, you will always struggle to read the newspaper righteously! If you insist on taking the short view of things you will be forever frustrated, confused, and angry.

This principle is especially seen in Revelation 19:1-8 where we read of the perspective of those surrounding the heavenly throne of God. Their declaration of praise is in response to the judgment on Babylon described in Revelation 18. God is to be praised and all power and glory ascribed to him precisely because he has 'judged the great prostitute' (Rev. 19:2). Far from the outpouring of wrath and the destruction of his enemies being a blight on God's character or a reason to question his love and kindness (as unbelievers so often suggest), they are the very reason for worship! God's judgments against the unbelieving world system and its followers are 'true and just' (see 15:3-4 and 16:5-7), for the harlot was corrupting (cf. 17:1-5; 18:3,7-9) the earth with her immorality, thereby meriting divine vengeance.

As if once were not enough, now 'once more' the cry of 'Hallelujah!' is sounded (vv. 3-4). This verdict is echoed (note their 'Amen', a formal expression of ratification and endorsement) by the twenty-four elders and four living creatures.

Again, a 'great multitude' shouts forth its praise (v. 6). Surely this is the same group, whoever they may be, that began this worship service in verse 1. Only here their voice is even louder (like the 'roar of many waters' and 'mighty peals of thunder'), gradually increasing as they reflect more deeply on the reasons why God is worthy of praise (as stated in v. 2 and all of chapter 18).

(3) A contemplative focus on heaven produces the fruit of endurance and perseverance now. The strength to endure *present suffering* is the fruit of meditating on *future satisfaction!* This is the clear message of several texts such as Matthew 5:11-12; Romans 8:17-18,23,25b; Hebrews 13:13-14; and 1 Peter 1:3-8.

Romans 8:18 is Paul's declaration that 'the sufferings of this present time are not worth comparing with the glory that is to be revealed to us.' We do not lose heart because we contemplate the unseen things of the future and nourish our souls with the truth that whatever we endure on this earth is producing a glory far beyond all comparison! Christians are not asked to treat pain as though it were pleasure, or grief as though it were joy, but to bring all earthly adversity into comparison with heavenly glory and thereby be strengthened to endure. The exhortation in Hebrews 13:13-14 to willingly bear the reproach of Christ is grounded in the expectation of a 'city that is to come', namely, the heavenly New Jerusalem.

Nowhere is this principle better seen than in 2 Corinthians 4:16-18. Gazing at the grandeur of heavenly glory transforms our value system. In the light of what is 'eternal', what we face now is only 'momentary'. Suffering appears *prolonged* only in the absence of an eternal perspective. The 'affliction' of this life is regarded as *light* when compared with the 'weight' of that 'glory' yet to come. It is *burdensome* only when we lose sight of our heavenly future. The key to success in suffering, as odd as that sounds, is in taking the long view. Only when juxtaposed with the endless ages of eternal bliss does suffering in this life become tolerable.

There is yet another contrast to be noted. In verse 18 Paul juxtaposes 'transient' things 'that are seen' with 'eternal' things 'that are unseen.' Note especially the connection between verses 18 and 16. Our 'inner nature' is being renewed *as we look* or *while we look* at the unseen, eternal things of the age to come. If you don't 'look' you won't change! The process of renewal only occurs *as the believer looks to things as yet unseen*. As we fix the gaze of our hearts on the glorious hope of the age to come, God progressively renews our inner being, notwithstanding the simultaneous decay of our outer frame! Inner renewal does not happen automatically or mechanically. Transformation happens only *as* or *provided that* we 'look not to the things that are seen, but to the things that are unseen' (v. 18).

Paul is here describing in his own terms the battle for the mind of mankind. On what shall we set our sights (cf. Col. 3:1-4)? To what shall we give our allegiance? On what shall we meditate and ponder and focus? At no time in history has this been a more relevant issue given recent statistics concerning television viewing habits in our country. The typical American teenager today watches 18,000 murders and 35,000 commercials before he/she graduates from high school! Someone has calculated that by the time they reach the age of sixty-five, they will have spent *ten years* watching TV!

(4) Nothing exerts such purifying power on the heart as does a contemplative focus on heaven. Meditation on the unseen glories of heaven energizes the heart to say 'No' to fleshly desires. This is the clear witness of Colossians 3:1-4; I John 3:2-3; and 2 Peter 3:11-13.

(5) Finally, concentrating on the glory of heaven teaches us about the essence of true religion. The way to learn the quintessential nature of anything, said Edwards, is to look closely where that thing is found in its highest and purest expression. To know true religion, therefore, we must look at it in its heavenly expression, and in doing so we discover that religion consists preeminently in holy affections:

> If we can learn anything of the state of heaven from the Scripture, the love and joy that the saints have there, is exceeding great and vigorous; impressing the heart with the strongest and most lively sensation, of inexpressible sweetness, mightily moving, animating, and engaging them, making them like to a flame of fire. And if such love and joy be not affections, then the word 'affection' is of no use in language. Will any say, that the saints in heaven, in beholding the face of their Father, and the glory of their Redeemer, and contemplating his wonderful works, and particularly his laying down his life for them, have their hearts nothing moved and affected, by all which they behold or consider?[2]

Heaven's Irresistible Appeal

We're now ready to concentrate on the nature of our heavenly experience and the beatific vision of God for which we long. This is what gives heaven its irresistible appeal and its contemporary impact.

Heaven is characterized by the increase of joy. Heaven is not simply about the reality or experience of joy, but its *eternal increase*. The blessedness of the beauty of heaven is progressive, incremental, and incessantly expansive.

The happiness of heaven is not like the steady, placid state of a mountain lake where barely a ripple disturbs the tranquility of its water. Heaven is more akin to the surging, swelling waves of the Mississippi at flood stage. With each passing day there is an increase in the level of water. And as the rain of revelation and insight and discovery continues to fall throughout the endless ages of eternity, so the water level of love and joy and happiness rises higher and higher, never to abate or to any degree diminish.

In the summer of 2002 the central region of Texas, just north of San Antonio, was hit by a devastating flood, a tragedy of almost incalculable proportions. My ears perked up one night when the television news anchor reported that the flood waters had finally receded. The river had crested the night before and people were now able to return to their homes (or at least what was left of them). Although this was certainly good news for them, you will never hear anything of the sort in heaven, at least when it comes to the 'river' of God's 'delights' (Psalm 36:8). The waters of divine knowledge in the age to come bring, not devastation, but delight. The heavenly river of revelation will never crest! The waters of our enjoyment will suffer no such limitations. 'Recede' is a word absent from the heavenly dictionary.

Look with me at what Paul says in Ephesians 2:7. God made us alive together with Christ and raised us up with him 'so that in the coming ages he might show the immeasurable riches of his grace in kindness toward us in Christ Jesus'. This text deserves our careful attention.

Making us alive in Christ and setting us free from the guilt and bondage of spiritual death was only the *penultimate* purpose of God. The *ultimate* motivation in God's heart for saving lost souls was so that they might become, throughout all eternity, trophies on display for all to see the magnificence and the surpassing riches of God's grace in kindness in Christ!

Paul's language is carefully chosen. He employs the plural 'ages' to accentuate the stunning reality that redeemed sinners will bear ceaseless witness to the mercy of God, both now and hereafter. Like waves incessantly crashing on the shore, one upon another, so the ages of eternity future will, in endless succession, echo the celebration of sinners saved by grace, all to the glory of God. There will not be in heaven a one-time momentary display of God's goodness, but an everlasting, ever-increasing infusion and impartation of divine kindness that intensifies with every passing moment.

To emphasize both the extravagance and inexhaustible plenitude of God's display of grace, Paul makes four points.

First, God is going to put on a continuing and perpetual public display of his 'grace' toward us! Heaven is not one grand, momentary flash of excitement followed by an eternity of boredom. Heaven is not going to be an endless series of earthly re-runs! There will be a new episode of divine grace every day! A new revelation every moment of some heretofore unseen aspect of the unfathomable complexity of divine compassion. A new and fresh disclosure of an implication or consequence of God's mercy, every day. A novel and stunning explanation of the meaning of what God has done for us, without end.

Second, it isn't merely his grace, but the wealth or 'riches' of his grace. God isn't simply gracious: his grace is deep, wide, high, wealthy, plentiful, abounding, infinitely replenishing.

Third, as if mere grace weren't enough, Paul refers to the

'immeasurable' or surpassing riches of his grace! His grace cannot be quantified. His mercy exceeds calculation.

Finally, one particular aspect of God's grace is going to be
uniquely highlighted and experienced: his 'kindness'! There is a
deeply passionate and emotional dynamic in God's gracious
affection for us that entails tenderness and gentleness and
longsuffering and joy and heartfelt compassion.

Ever-Increasing Grace

Will there ever be an end to this grace? Does it suffer from
entropy? Will it ultimately evaporate? Is there a specified quantity
to God's kindness that will slowly diminish and someday run
dry? The point of Paul's effusive language is to emphasize that
the grace of God in Christ is endlessly infinite, endlessly
complex, endlessly deep, endlessly new, endlessly fresh, endlessly
profound. God is infinite. Therefore, so too are his attributes.
Throughout the ages to come, forever and ever, we will be the
recipients each instant of an ever increasing and more stunning,
more fascinating, and thus inescapably more enjoyable display
of God's grace than before.

With that unending and ever-increasing *display* will come
an unending and ever-increasing *discovery* on our part of more
of the depths and greatness of God's grace. We will learn and
grasp and comprehend more of the height and depth and width
and breadth of his saving love. We will see ever new and always
fresh displays and manifestations of his kindness. The knowledge
we gain when we enter heaven will forever grow and deepen and
expand and intensify and multiply.

We will constantly be more amazed with God, more in love
with God, and thus ever more relishing his presence and our
relationship with him. Our experience of God will never reach
it consummation. We will never finally arrive, as if upon reaching

a peak we discover there is nothing beyond. Our experience of God will never become stale. It will deepen and develop, intensify and amplify, unfold and increase, broaden and balloon. Our relishing and rejoicing in God will sharpen and spread and extend and progress and mature and flower and blossom and widen and stretch and swell and snowball and inflate and lengthen and augment and advance and proliferate and accumulate and accelerate and multiply and heighten and reach a crescendo that will even then be only the beginning of an eternity of new and fresh insights into the majesty of who God is!

Ever-Increasing Knowledge

Will our knowledge increase in heaven as 'time' passes? Consider the angels. They are perfect and sinless, yet their knowledge increases and their joy intensifies. They desire to look into the things of redemption (I Peter I:I2) and rejoice when a sinner repents (Luke 15:7,10). Clearly, growth of insight and new grounds for joy characterize angelic experience in heaven. If this be true of them, why not of us?

There never will come a time in heaven when we will know all that can be known or see or feel or experience or enjoy all that can be enjoyed. We will never plumb the depths of gratification in God nor reach its end. Our satisfaction and delight and joy in him are subject to incessant increase. When it comes to heavenly euphoria, words such as termination and cessation and expiration and finality are utterly inappropriate and inapplicable.

One of the greatest misconceptions of heaven is that it is static, unchanging, and immutable, as if to say that all we get we get all at once, at the beginning. The idea many have is that we are transformed at its inception as much as we ever will be. No. But to think that the happiness of heaven is unchanging minimizes its glory.

If our ideas and thoughts of God increase in heaven, then so also must the joy and delight and fascination which those ideas and thoughts generate. We enter heaven with a finite number of ideas about God, with obvious limits on what we know of him. There is no indication that everything that can be known of God will be known all at once and forever. How could a finite being *ever* know all there is to know of an infinite being?

With increased knowledge comes intensified love. As understanding grows, so too does affection and fascination. With each new insight comes more joy, which serves only to stoke the fires of celebration around the throne. All of this accelerates our growth in holiness. When the soul is filled with ever-increasing depths of knowledge, love, joy, and worship, the more it is conformed to the image of Christ. In other words, the more we like God the more like God we become!

New ideas, new revelation, new insights, new applications, together with new connections between one idea and another all lead to deeper appreciation for God and thus fuel the flames of worship. And just when you think you're going to *explode* if you learn anything more or hear anything fresh or see anything new, God expands your heart and stretches your mind and broadens your emotions and extends every faculty to take in yet more and more and more, and so it goes forever and ever. Says Edwards:

> Therefore, their knowledge will increase to eternity; and if their knowledge, doubtless their holiness. For as they increase in the knowledge of God and of the works of God, the more they will see of his excellency; and the more they see of his excellency ... the more will they love him; and the more they love God, the more delight and happiness ... will they have in him.[3]

The basis for knowing this to be true is the biblical reality of *God's inexhaustible plenitude.*

We must never forget that even in heaven only God is immutable or unchanging. We are ever subject to greater transformation and improvement. But it is always a change from one stage of glory and knowledge and holiness to the next higher stage of glory and knowledge and holiness. It is one thing to be free of imperfection, but another to experience perfection perfectly. We will be perfect in heaven from the first moment we arrive in that we will be free from defect, free from sin, free from moral corruption and selfishness. But that perfection is finite, because we are finite. It is always subject to expansion. There is change, but always for the better!

Heaven is not simply the eradication of earthly sin and imperfection. To say that in heaven I will no longer hate God is not the same as loving him perfectly. My love can be free from corruption and selfishness without being as perfect and intense as is possible. To say that my love for God is absolutely perfect and cannot be improved upon implies that I know everything that can be known of him and that I know it in exhaustive detail. This is worse than absurd, it's arrogant.

All aspects of our 'perfection' in heaven admit of degrees precisely because we are and always will be finite. Whatever is finite has boundaries and boundaries, by definition, are capable of being exceeded and extended. Knowledge that is perfect and free from error is not necessarily comprehensive. Our happiness will be perfect in that it will be entirely free from trouble and trial and evil, but that perfection, as strange as it may sound, is always subject to improvement.

Now Counts Forever

To think that everyone in heaven is equally knowledgeable, equally holy, equally capable of enjoying God, is to argue that the progress we make now on earth is irrelevant to our heavenly state. But we are often exhorted to do things now precisely because it will build up and increase for us treasure in heaven.[4] Not everyone responds to these commands in the same way or to the same degree or with the same measure of faithfulness. Thus people will enter heaven at differing degrees of holiness, love, and joy. All will be subject to increase and expansion based on the depth and measure of our development here on earth. What we do and know and achieve now, by God's grace, will have eternal consequences.

Your capacity for happiness in heaven is shaped by the development and refinement and depth of your capacity on earth. What we do now is not discarded once we enter eternity. What we learn now is not erased in heaven. Nothing in Scripture leads us to believe that everyone will be instantaneously, equally, and exhaustively educated at the inauguration of our heavenly existence. What we experience in joy and understanding and insight now is not destroyed, but is the foundation on which all our eternal experience and growth is based.

Ever-Increasing Joy

If God's desire is to be glorified, then it seems that he must do whatever is necessary that his glory may be seen and honored in ever increasing ways. Perhaps in heaven God will enlarge our intellectual capacity to know him and heighten the sensitivity of our affections to love him and transform every faculty of soul, spirit, and body to enjoy him to a degree never before attained or imagined. Our minds and wills and emotions and bodies and spirits will no longer be limited by the corruptions of the flesh or the boundaries of earth.[5]

But if we are never able to reach consummate perfection and complete knowledge of God, won't we feel frustrated and disappointed and anxious? No. Because *there will never be a time when we are denied what we desire.* Happiness consists in part in the satisfaction of desire. In heaven, with each desire there is fulfillment. We will desire only what is good and righteous and honoring to God, and it would be hell if such desire were left unsatisfied. Each new desire is but a fitting prelude to the delight that comes with its satisfaction.

Frustration and disappointment and anxiety are the fruit of not attaining what your heart desires. But in heaven whatever we want we get. If we want more knowledge, we'll learn. If we want more enjoyment, we get it. *With each new desire comes a corresponding satisfaction.* And with each new satisfaction, with each new discovery, yet unseen and unexperienced possibilities of enjoying and knowing God will emerge to which our hearts will reach in desire, which desire will in turn be fulfilled, which in turn will open up new vistas not yet attained, which when desired will then be fulfilled and satisfied, and on and on forever and ever.

Often people doubt the happiness of heaven to come because of their misery in this world. They find that divine providence seems to deprive them of happiness now. What reason, then, do they have for believing that they will have happiness later? This question fails to realize that God limits the happiness and pleasure we have now precisely so we might not become attached to this world or dependent upon it or fearful of leaving it (dying), as well as to stir in our hearts a longing and yearning and holy anticipation for what is yet to come.

That we will grow in happiness in heaven seems evident from the fact that the ideas and thoughts and insights into the nature and work of God will forever increase. We are mistaken to think that what we perceive to be beautiful now is the limit or boundary for what will be beautiful in heaven. With a new heavens and a new earth there will undoubtedly be new colors, new combinations, new hues, new depths of radiance, together with new faculties of mind, sense and spirit to apprehend new disclosures of God's infinite splendor.

What We Won't See There

Three texts in Revelation tell us who and what will be absent in heaven. In 21:4 we see that no tears of grief, no death or sorrow or pain will be present. In 21:8 we are assured that no one who is cowardly, lying, or unbelieving will be present, or murderers, or anything abominable, immoral, or idolatrous. And, as if to sum up, we are told in 21:27 that nothing unclean will be allowed to enter.

Think of the implications of what is being said! When we get to heaven there will be nothing that is abrasive, irritating, agitating, or hurtful. Nothing harmful, hateful, upsetting or unkind. Nothing sad, bad, or mad. Nothing harsh, impatient, ungrateful or unworthy. Nothing weak, or sick, or broken or foolish. Nothing deformed, degenerate, depraved or disgusting. Nothing polluted, pathetic, poor or putrid. Nothing dark, dismal, dismaying or degrading. Nothing blameworthy, blemished, blasphemous or blighted. Nothing faulty, faithless, frail or fading. Nothing grotesque or grievous, hideous or insidious. Nothing illicit or illegal, lascivious or lustful. Nothing marred or mutilated, misaligned or misinformed. Nothing nasty or naughty, offensive or odious. Nothing rancid or rude, soiled or spoiled. Nothing tawdry or tainted, tasteless or tempting. Nothing vile or vicious, wasteful or wanton!

What We Will See There

Wherever you turn your eyes you will see nothing but glory and grandeur and beauty and brightness and purity and perfection and splendor and satisfaction and sweetness and salvation and majesty and marvel and holiness and happiness.

We will see only and all that is adorable and affectionate, beautiful and bright, brilliant and bountiful, delightful and delicious, delectable and dazzling, elegant and exciting, fascinating and fruitful, glorious and grand, gracious and good, happy and holy, healthy and whole, joyful and jubilant, lovely and luscious, majestic and marvelous, opulent and overwhelming, radiant and resplendent, splendid and sublime, sweet and savoring, tender and tasteful, euphoric and unified!

Why will it be all these things? Because we will be looking at God (see Matt. 5:8; John 17:24; Heb. 12:14; Rev. 22:4). This beatific vision will be utterly *transparent*. Now we 'see through a glass, darkly' (1 Cor. 13 KJV), obscured and blurry. But God will one day unveil himself in all his resplendent brilliance, glory, and clarity for us to behold.

This beatific vision of God will be utterly *transcendent*, and will in every conceivable way outstrip and exceed and transcend the glory and beauty and majesty of anything we have ever seen on this earth. Hence we will never grow weary or bored with looking at God.

This beatific vision of God will be utterly *transforming*. Moses saw the 'back', or hindquarters of God, if you will (see Exodus 33:19-23). This resulted in a glowing brilliance on his face that terrified the people, from which they turned away. The dazzling brilliance that transformed Moses' face was too much for them to bear, yet this came from his beholding the back of God, not his face! Our eternal destiny is to see him face to face. What will it be for us to bask in the radiant glory and refulgent beauty of His divine countenance!

What We Will Do There

For one thing, we will no longer enjoy sin! For example, envy and covetousness and spite, all those things which fill our hearts when we see others exceeding us in prosperity, surpassing us in success, elevated beyond us in worldly affairs, will be forever absent from heaven.

Hardly anything will bring you more joy than to see other saints with greater rewards than you, experiencing greater glory than you, given greater authority than you! There will be no jealousy or pride to fuel your unhealthy competitiveness. There will be no greed to energize your race to get more than everyone else. *You will then delight only in delighting in the delight of others. Their achievement will be your greatest joy. Their success will be your highest happiness.* You will truly rejoice with those who rejoice. Envy comes from lack. But in heaven there is no lack. Whatever you need, you get. Whatever desires may arise, they are satisfied.

The fact that some are more holy and more happy than others will not diminish the joy of the latter. There will be perfect humility and perfect resignation to God's will in heaven, hence no resentment or bitterness. Also, those higher in holiness will, precisely because they are holy, be more humble. The essence of holiness is humility! The very vice that might incline them to look condescendingly on those lower than themselves is nowhere present. It is precisely because they are more holy that they are so very humble and thus incapable of arrogance and elitism.

They will not strut or boast or use their higher degrees of glory to humiliate or harm those lower. Those who know more of God will, because of that knowledge, think more lowly and humbly of themselves. They will be more aware of the grace that accounts for their holiness than those who know and experience less of God, hence, they will be more ready to serve and to yield and to go low and to defer.

Some people in heaven will be happier than others. But this is no reason for sadness or anger. In fact, *it will serve only to*

*make you happier to see that others are more happy than you!
Your happiness will increase when you see that the happiness of others has exceeded your own.* Why? Because love dominates in heaven and love is rejoicing in the increase of the happiness of others. To love someone is to desire their greatest joy. As their joy increases, so too does yours in them. If their joy did not increase, neither would yours. We struggle with this because now on earth our thoughts and desires and motives are corrupted by sinful self-seeking, competitiveness, envy, jealousy, and resentment. Edwards again summed it up best:

> *How soon do earthly lovers come to an end of their discoveries of each other's beauty; how soon do they see all that is to be seen! ... And how happy is that love, in which there is an eternal progress in all these things; wherein new beauties are continually discovered, and more and more loveliness, and in which we shall forever increase in beauty ourselves; where we shall be made capable of finding out and giving, and shall receive, more and more endearing expressions of love forever: our union will become more close, and communication more intimate.*[6]

In this life it's often hard to be happy when you hurt. In heaven, with new and glorified bodies, there will be no fatigue, pain, discomfort, chronic aches or itches. There will be only pure physical pleasure with no bodily obstacles to diminish our ability to see and feel and hear and touch and taste and smell the glories of paradise. Now, on earth, physical pleasure often competes with spiritual happiness, but in heaven they are one! The physical and emotional and intellectual pleasures of heaven will infinitely exceed the most ecstatic of physical and sensual pleasures on earth.

There will be no bodily lusts to pull you down, no physical fatigue to cloud your mind, no wicked impulses against which you must fight, no dullness of heart to hold you back, no lethargy of soul to slow you down, no weakness of will to keep you in bondage, no lack of energy to love someone else, no absence of passion to pursue what is holy.

Insofar as our bodies will be glorified in heaven and thus delivered of weakness and frailty and obscurity and our senses all heightened and magnified and their capacity to see, touch, feel, hear, and smell greatly increased and no longer hindered by disease or distraction, our experience will be indescribably joyful. 'Every perceptive faculty shall be an inlet of delight.'[7]

What We Will Hear There

One of the greatest joys of heaven will be the exalted sound of perfected souls singing their joyful praises to God. 'The best, most beautiful, and most perfect way that we have of expressing a sweet concord of mind to each other,' said Edwards, 'is by music.'[8] Thus in heaven, he continued, it is probable 'that the glorified saints, after they have again received their bodies, will have ways of expressing the concord of their minds by some other emanations than sounds, of which we cannot conceive, that will be vastly more proportionate, harmonious and delightful than the nature of sounds is capable of; and the music they will make will be in a medium capable of modulations in an infinitely more nice, exact and fine proportion than our gross air, and with organs as much more adapted to such proportions.'[9] In heaven, 'there shall be no string out of tune to cause any jar in the harmony of that world, no unpleasant note to cause any discord.'[10]

Finally, you need never live in fear that any heavenly joy will ever be lost or taken away! We struggle to enjoy life now from fear that it will soon end. We hesitate to savor what little happiness we have for fear that it may be taken away. We hold back and hedge our bets and restrain our souls, knowing that disaster may soon come, economic recession may begin, physical health may deteriorate, someone may die, or something unforeseen may surprise us and take it all away. *But not in heaven! Never! The beauty and joy and glory and delight and satisfaction and purity will never ever end, but only increase and grow and expand and multiply!*

All this, for hell-deserving sinners!

Oh, that God might hasten the day when our relishing and rejoicing in him reach their consummate expression!

---

[1] The Greek word, *politeuma*, translated 'citizenship', has the sense of a dynamic, transforming force. It is a power that shapes how we think and feel and react and choose.

[2] Jonathan Edwards, *Religious Affections*, The Works of Jonathan Edwards, Volume 2. Edited by John E. Smith (New Haven: Yale University Press, 1969), p. 114.

[3] Jonathan Edwards, *The Miscellanies*, The Works of Jonathan Edwards, Volume 13. Edited by Thomas A. Schafer (New Haven: Yale University Press, 1994), no. 105, pp. 275-76.

[4] At least three things determine degrees of glory in heaven. (1) Degrees of holiness on earth. See Heb. 10:35; James 1:12; Luke 14:11; Matt. 18:4. (2) Degrees of self-denial and sufferings endured on earth. See Matt. 5:10-12; 19:29; 2 Tim. 2:11-12; 1 Pt. 4:13. (3) Degrees of good deeds done in the body. See Jer. 17:10; Dan. 12:3; 1 Thess. 2:19; John 4:35-36; 1 Cor. 3:10-15; 2 Cor. 5:10.

[5] 'And without doubt,' said Edwards, 'God can contrive mat-

ter so that there shall be other sort of proportions, that may be quite of a different kind, and may raise another sort of pleasure in the sense, and in a manner to us inconceivable, that shall be vastly more ravishing and exquisite. ...Our animal spirits will also be capable of immensely more, fine and exquisite proportions in their motions than now they are, being so gross' (*The Miscellanies*, The Works of Jonathan Edwards, Volume 13. Edited by Thomas A. Schafer [New Haven: Yale University Press, 1994], no. 182, p. 328).

[6] Jonathan Edwards, *The Miscellanies*, The Works of Jonathan Edwards, Volume 13. Edited by Thomas A. Schafer (New Haven: Yale University Press, 1994), no. 198, pp. 336-37.

[7] Ibid., no. 721, p. 350.

[8] Jonathan Edwards, *The Miscellanies*, The Works of Jonathan Edwards, Volume 13. Edited by Thomas A. Schafer (New Haven: Yale University Press, 1994), no. 188, p. 331.

[9] Ibid.

[10] Jonathan Edwards, 'Heaven is a World of Love,' in *Ethical Writings*, The Works of Jonathan Edwards, Volume 8. Edited by Paul Ramsey (New Haven: Yale University Press, 1989), p. 371.

Epilogue

The cover of *Time* magazine of 1 July 2002 caught my eye. In bold print were the words: *The Bible & the Apocalypse, Why more Americans are reading and talking about The End of the World.*

The article that followed was an attempt to account for the increased curiosity concerning when the world might come to an end as well as the staggering sales of the Tim LaHaye and Jerry Jenkins fictional series, *Left Behind.* On reading this article one might think the end of history is all about the Antichrist or Israel or the rapture or 666 or any number of other themes associated with the theology of dispensationalism. But it isn't.

The end of history is all about the beauty of God. The consummation is all about the admiration and adoration of our Lord Jesus Christ as he is to be revealed in heaven. I've heard and read countless explanations for the second coming of Jesus, but none that has adequately grasped the ultimate reason for his return. The inspired rationale is found in Paul's second letter to the Thessalonian church. Jesus is coming back, said

Paul, 'to be glorified in his saints, and to be marveled at among all who have believed' (2 Thess. 1:10).

I need to return momentarily to my love affair with prepositions. Here Paul says that Jesus will be glorified 'in' his saints and marveled at 'among' all who believe. This calls for careful thought. After considerable study, I think John Stott best captures the essence of Paul's emphasis. He writes:

> So how will the coming Lord Jesus be glorified in relation to his people? Not 'among' them, as if they will be the theatre or stadium in which he appears; nor 'by' them, as if they will be the spectators, the audience who watch and worship; nor 'through' or 'by means of' them, as if they will be mirrors which reflect his image and glory; but rather 'in' them, as if they will be a filament, which itself glows with light and heat when the electric current passes through it.[1]

Stott's point is that we will not only see Christ's glory, we will be enveloped within it, engulfed by its surging splendor, and made experiential participants of it. And that for eternity! We will not glow with his glory for a moment, only to diminish yet again into the darkness of self and sin. 'We will be radically and permanently changed, being transformed into his likeness. And in our transformation his glory will be seen in us, for we will glow for ever with the glory of Christ.'[2]

All of this will lead to one passionate, universal response among Christians to Christ: *Marvel!* This glorious Greek word emphasizes the experience of being overwhelmingly astonished and utterly astounded and absolutely amazed and joyfully surprised and fully filled with wonder and awe. That's why he's coming back. All else is subservient to that end. Whatever events may transpire at the end of time, whoever may arise and how ever many may fall, whether it be near at hand or centuries afar,

Jesus is coming to be seen in his saints in the beauty and splendor of his eternal majesty.

The apostle does not write of Christ's return to add fuel to our apocalyptic speculations but to awaken us to the purifying power of seeing him in all his unparalleled splendor (see I John 3:1-3). History has taken many turns and suffered what appear to us to be countless setbacks in moments of both great triumph and horrid tragedy. But on that day when Christ is revealed from heaven we will see how its ultimate purpose has been preparation for the unveiling of divine beauty. Then we will see him! No longer obscure, no longer through a glass darkly, but in all the ecstasy of beholding him face to face and enjoying him, to his glory, forever and ever.

This same breathtaking truth is found in Matthew 25:31 where we read that Jesus will return 'in his *glory*' to 'sit on his *glorious* throne.' And again in Titus 2:13 the second coming is nothing less than the 'appearing of the *glory* of our great God and Savior Jesus Christ.' Jesus himself obviously knew this, which explains why he prayed that his disciples 'see' his '*glory*' (John 17:24).

So what does it mean to say he will return and appear in *glory*? Picture this. Jesus will come bathed in radiant splendor, enveloped within an atmosphere of indescribable brilliance, surrounded by the ear-piercing praise of angels and saints. Scintillating light shining from his eyes. Irresistible power pouring from his hands. None will deny his beauty or escape its transforming energy.

But how can this be good news if we cannot *now* see him? Can we still be changed by his beauty as we await with unbridled anticipation the glory of that day? Yes, for as Peter said, 'Though you have not seen him, you love him. Though you do not now see him, you believe in him and rejoice with joy that is inexpressible and filled with glory' (I Pet. I:8).

Sufficient is the revelation of his beauty now, in Scripture, in creation, in providence, and in the church, that our passion for him *can* flourish to the defeat of sin and our joy in him *can* increase to the glory of his name.

A Gracious and Supernatural Light

I conclude with this. The apprehension of spiritual beauty in Jesus and the sweet transformation of life it brings is not, in the final analysis, the fruit of human effort. The reason why Christians alone experience God as he is revealed in Jesus is due to the sovereign initiative of divine grace. There has been infused within them by the regenerating work of the Holy Spirit a new taste, a new sense of the sweetness and beauty and grandeur of God in Christ.

When the light of spiritual illumination shined in the soul of Peter, imparting to him the knowledge that Jesus is the Messiah, the Son of the Living God, it was our Father in heaven to whom credit was given (Matthew 16:16-17; see also 11:25-30). Neither flesh and blood nor anything human nature in all its effort or education could produce accounted for Peter's saving insight. This was the revelatory work of God the Father, through the Holy Spirit, and for this reason Peter is deemed blessed.

It's no less true for you and me now than for Peter then. To whatever degree we know and see and savor and enjoy the revelation of divine beauty in Jesus, it is the gracious work of God. Thank you, Lord.

---

[1] John Stott, *The Gospel & the End of Time: The Message of 1 & 2 Thessalonians* (Downers Grove: IVP, 1991), p. 149.

[2] Ibid., pp. 149-50.

Other books of interest
from
Christian Focus

Why do I Suffer?

Suffering and the Sovereignty of God

John Currid

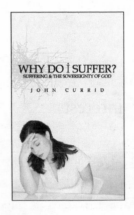

Why *does* God allow suffering?

It's a question that, in one form or another rears its ugly head time and again. Whether it comes from someone who has just lost a loved one, been diagnosed with an incurable illness or even just surveyed the plight of the poor in the third world. Every terrorist attack or world disaster raises the question – Where was God in this?

The question is one that has dogged Christians down the ages. A number of answers have been offered – and indeed all worldviews attempt their own response. John Currid brings Biblical teaching to bear. God does work in suffering, he is not a worried observer unwilling or unable to intervene, rather he has a purpose at work and is in control.

As Abraham said "Shall not the Judge of all the Earth do right?"

Grasping that truth will help us as we face the future and ensure that when we are next faced with that most tricky of questions we will know where to begin.

John Currid is Carl McMurray Professor of Old Testament at Reformed Theological Seminary, Jackson, Mississippi. He is a prolific author whose books include well received, multivolume commentaries on Genesis, Exodus and soon Leviticus.

ISBN 1-85792-954-3

Song of a Satisfied Soul

Finding the Life You're Longing for from Psalm 23

John A. Kitchen

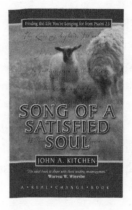

'The ideal book to share with those needing encouragement.'

Warren W. Wiersbe

'Shot through with vivid illustrations and stories, "The Song of a Satisfied Soul" is going to end up at bedsides, in hip pockets, and handbags, and on preachers' desks.'

Richard Bewes
All Souls Church, London

We all long for satisfaction. More often than not dashed hopes and frustrated efforts leave us wondering if it is a phantom appetite - forever defying fulfillment. No sooner do we achieve a major goal in life than another immediately presents itself – leaving us in a perpetual chase after contentment.

In the 23rd Psalm God lifts before us the *Song of the Satisfied Soul*. It's the promise of a life better than you've dreamt possible. God offers us the intimacy of a personal relationship with Himself. God Himself is our song, the singer, and the substance of the *Song of the Satisfied Soul*.

True satisfaction in life is found not when all want is removed, but when above all we want Christ.

John A. Kitchen is a Pastor from Ohio who has previously authored *Embracing Authority* (ISBN 1-85792-715-X) – a counter-cultural look at how Christians should view authority.

ISBN 1-85792-942-X

Christian Focus Publications

publishes books for all ages.

Our mission statement –

STAYING FAITHFUL

In dependence upon God we seek to help make His infallible Word, the Bible, relevant. Our aim is to ensure that the Lord Jesus Christ is presented as the only hope to obtain forgiveness of sin, live a useful life and look forward to heaven with Him.

REACHING OUT

Christ's last command requires us to reach out to our world with His gospel. We seek to help fulfill that by publishing books that point people towards Jesus and help them develop a Christ-like maturity. We aim to equip all levels of readers for life, work, ministry and mission.

Books in our adult range are published in three imprints.

Christian Focus contains popular works including biographies, commentaries, basic doctrine and Christian living. Our children's books are also published in this imprint.

Mentor focuses on books written at a level suitable for Bible College and seminary students, pastors, and other serious readers. The imprint includes commentaries, doctrinal studies, examination of current issues and church history.

Christian Heritage contains classic writings from the past.

Christian Focus Publications, Ltd
Geanies House, Fearn,
Ross-shire, Scotland,
IV20 ITW, United Kingdom
info@christianfocus.com

For details of our titles visit us on our website
www.christianfocus.com